What Can I Do Now?

Fashion

Books in the
***What Can I Do Now?* Series**

Art
Computers
Engineering, Second Edition
Fashion
Health Care
Music
Nursing, Second Edition
Radio and Television, Second Edition
Safety and Security, Second Edition
Sports, Second Edition

What Can I Do Now?

Fashion

Ferguson Publishing
An imprint of Infobase Publishing

What Can I Do Now? Fashion

Ferguson
An imprint of Infobase Publishing
132 West 31st Street
New York NY 10001

ISBN-10: 0-8160-6029-0
ISBN-13: 978-0-8160-6029-0

Library of Congress Cataloging-in-Publication Data
What can I do now? : Fashion.
p. cm.
Includes index.
ISBN 0-8160-6029-0 (hc : alk. paper)
1. Fashion—Vocational guidance—Juvenile literature. 2. Clothing trade—Vocational guidance—Juvenile literature. I. J.G. Ferguson Publishing Company.
TT507.W4445 2007
746.9'2023—dc22 2006029963

Ferguson books are available at special discounts when purchased in bulk quantities for businesses, associations, institutions, or sales promotions. Please call our Special Sales Department in New York at (212) 967-8800 or (800) 322-8755.

You can find Ferguson on the World Wide Web at http://www.fergpubco.com

Text design by Kerry Casey
Cover design by Takeshi Takahashi

Printed in the United States of America

VB FOF 10 9 8 7 6 5 4 3 2 1

This book is printed on acid-free paper.

All links and Web addresses were checked and verified to be correct at the time of publication. Because of the dynamic nature of the Web, some addresses and links may have changed since publication and may no longer be valid.

Contents

Introduction

If you are considering a career in fashion—which presumably you are since you're reading this book—you must realize that the better informed you are from the start, the better your chances of having a successful, satisfying career.

There is absolutely no reason to wait until you get out of high school to "get serious" about a career. That doesn't mean you have to make a firm, undying commitment right now. One of the biggest fears most people face at some point (sometimes more than once) is choosing the right career, and frankly, many people don't "choose" at all. They take a job because they need one, and all of a sudden 10 years have gone by and they wonder why they're stuck doing something they hate. Don't be one of those people! You have the opportunity right now—while you're still in high school and still relatively unencumbered with major adult responsibilities—to explore, to experience, to try out a work path—(or several paths, if you're one of those overachieving types.) Wouldn't you really rather find out sooner than later that you're not cut out to be a fashion model after all, that you'd actually prefer to be a fashion designer? Or a fashion coordinator?

There are many ways to explore the field of fashion. This book gives you an idea of some of your options. The chapter "What Do I Need to Know About the Fashion Industry?" provides an overview of the field—a little history, where it's at today, and promises of the future; as well as a breakdown of its structure—how it's organized—and a glimpse of some of its many career options.

The "Careers" section includes 10 chapters, each describing in detail a specific fashion career: buyer and merchandiser, fashion coordinator, fashion designer, fashion illustrator, fashion agent, fashion photographer, fashion writer and editor, makeup artist, model, fashion stylist. These chapters rely heavily on firsthand accounts from real people on the job. They'll tell you the skills and personal qualities you need to have, as well as the ups and downs of the jobs. You'll also find out about educational requirements—including specific high school and college classes—advancement possibilities, related jobs, salary ranges, and the employment outlook.

Section 3: "Do It Yourself" urges you to take charge and start your own programs and activities where none exist—at school, in your community, or nationally.

The real meat of the book is in Section 4, "What Can I Do Right Now?" This is where you get busy and do something. "Get Involved" describes volunteer and intern positions, summer camps and summer college study, and other opportunities.

While this book is geared toward exploring fashion by jumping right in and doing it, there are plenty of other ways to get into the fashion mind-set. "Surf the Web" offers you a short annotated list of fashion Web sites where you can explore everything from job listings (start getting an idea of what employers are looking for now) to educational requirements to on-the-job accounts.

"Read a Book" is an annotated bibliography of books (some new, some old) and periodicals. If you're even remotely considering a career in fashion, reading a few books and checking out a few magazines is the easiest thing you can do. Don't stop with our list. Ask your librarian to point you to more fashion-related materials.

"Ask for Money" is a sampling of fashion scholarships and other financial aid. You need to be familiar with these because you're going to need money for school. You have to actively pursue scholarships; no one is going to come up to you in the hall one day and present you with a check because you're such a wonderful student. Applying for scholarships is work. It takes effort. And it must be done right and on time, often a year in advance of when you need the money.

"Look to the Pros" is the final chapter. It's a list of professional organizations that you can turn to for more information about accredited schools, education requirements, career descriptions, salary information, job listings, scholarships, and much more. Once you become a fashion student, you'll be able to join some of these. Time after time, professionals say that membership and active participation in a professional organization is one of the best ways to network (make valuable contacts) and gain recognition in your field.

High school can be a lot of fun. There are dances and football games; maybe you're in band or play a sport. Or maybe you hate school and are just biding your time until you graduate. Whatever your approach, take a minute to imagine your life five years from now. Ten years from now. Where will you be? What will you be doing? Whether you realize it or not, how you choose to spend your time now—studying, playing, watching TV, working at a fast food restaurant, hanging out—will have an impact on your future. Look at how you spend your time and ask yourself, "Where is this getting me?" If you can't come up with an answer, it's probably "nowhere." The choice is yours. It's up to you to choose your direction, because, after all, it's your life. You can do something about it right now!

SECTION 1

What Do I Need to Know About the Fashion Industry?

Ever since you were little, you had a passion for clothes—dresses, shoes, coats, and all accessories. You loved to dress dolls, and even made their clothes. Or maybe you've been known as a spiffy dresser. Your family and friends always turn to you for fashion advice—you always seem to know how to put clothes together to create a new look. Now you are seriously thinking of transferring this passion into a career. Do you have the chops to make it in an industry known for its fast-track competitiveness? If you are thinking of becoming a runway model, you'll need genetics on your side. To those not blessed with supermodel height, weight, and bone structure, there are plenty of other possibilities in the fashion industry. Fashion sense, along with a good education, work experience and training, inspiration, and a fair amount of luck will result in a rewarding career. Talented people are needed to design, sew, and create clothing, footwear, and other accessories. Photographers and stylists are needed to create fashion photography to entice consumers to buy the items. Fashion agents are important liaisons for models and businesses. Fashion coordinators are key to getting new trends off the ground from manufacturers and retail stores to the public. The possibilities are truly endless. It's up to you to make the most of your education and experience. Read on to learn more about this exciting and fascinating industry!

GENERAL INFORMATION

Clothing has always been a necessity for people throughout the world. In primitive times, clothing provided its wearer warmth and protection from the elements. Later civilizations began to produce more elaborate fabrics and from these fabrics made more ornate clothing. Yet the importance of clothing still centered on its functionality, which was reflected in clothing design and production. Over the centuries, as societies and economies became more established, clothing began to satisfy more complex needs. People began using clothing to express their personalities, indicate their rank or social standing, and enhance their looks. By the early 20th century the manufacturing of clothes had become the booming industry of fashion.

In the United States, New York City quickly became the country's fashion industry headquarters due to its proximity to the woolen mills of New England and the cotton mills of the South. More importantly, however, were the city's inexpensive workforces in the form of immigrant workers.

During the middle and later half of the century, designers broadened their focus from creating only expensive and glamorous fashions (called haute couture) to designing ready-to-wear collections. This trend allowed more people access to fashion, since such clothing was less expensive and more practical.

STRUCTURE OF THE INDUSTRY

Workers in many industries help to create the fashions we wear for business and pleasure.

Lingo to Learn

AMTEX: American Textile Partnership.

CAD/CAM: Computer-aided designing and computer-aided manufacturing.

chargeback: Financial penalty for infractions, such as errors in purchase orders or failure to deliver floor-ready merchandise.

cruisewear: Apparel designed for vacationing, originally for shipboard activities.

dressmaker: Custom tailor.

fabricated: Assembled, produced; as in fabricated textiles.

floor-ready: Clothing on hangers, prepared for presentation in the store.

grading: Adjusting pieces of a garment for various sizes.

made to measure: Custom-designed apparel.

National Textile Center: Consortium of universities involved in textile research.

parity: Equality; elimination of tariffs on goods from other countries.

preticket: Price tag applied to a garment by the apparel firm, showing retailers' price.

ready-to-wear: Apparel manufactured in preset sizes, not customized.

showing: Event held to display new designs and styles to buyers and media representatives.

subsector: A specific area of apparel, such as men's and boys' clothing.

sweatshop: Small, factories or workshops, that are crowded, unsanitary, and unsafe, especially from fire.

tannery: Facility where animal hides are cleaned and preserved in tannin solutions to make leather.

tannin: Chemical extracted from certain trees or plants and used to keep leather from decomposing.

workroom: Location where textiles are cut and assembled into garments.

WWD: *Women's Wear Daily;* periodical considered the clothing industry bible.

Textiles

The textile industry produces fabrics for clothing, as well as fabrics for home furnishings, carpeting, towels, and sheets; ribbons, webbings, and tapes for automobile seat belts and conveyor belts; textiles for parachutes, fire-resistant and bullet-resistant uniforms; and fabrics for disposable surgical masks, gowns, and sheets, among other products. The textile industry is the largest manufacturing industry in the United States, with approximately 489,000 employees. The industry is also one of the most diversified, employing people from numerous racial, ethnic, and economic backgrounds. Employees work in three major categories: research and development, production, and merchandising.

Apparel

The apparel industry produces almost all types of clothing for men, women, and children and is made up of thousands of manufacturers. Nearly every important apparel manufacturer has a sales office in New York City. This is where large retailers send their buyers and where industry-wide sales meetings are held each new season. In addition to their New York offices, apparel companies often contract much of their production to foreign workers to cut down on production and labor costs. A large number of apparel industry workers are women and minorities, accounting for almost a third of the workforce.

Design/Marketing/Support

This industry supports numerous workers with a variety of responsibilities—ranging from the designers who create new styles of clothing and accessories; the workers who market and advertise these designs via print publications, the Internet, and fashion shows; and the support professionals who organize fashion shows, represent models and other fashion professionals, and help models to look their best when they market new fashions.

CAREERS

The following paragraphs detail the exciting opportunities that are available in the fashion industry:

- *Advertising and sales promotion personnel* create demand for fashion products with a variety of communications tools. Methods used include television advertisements and ads in consumer and trade magazines. Other promotional activities include point-of-sale displays, attractive packaging, exhibits at fashion shows, and promotions within department stores.
- *Apparel industry workers* produce, maintain, or repair clothing and other consumer products made from cloth, leather, or fur. The three basic processes of garment production are cutting, sewing, and pressing. Apparel industry employees work primarily in manufacturing firms, though some are employed in retail establishments or laundries and dry cleaners. They may be involved in creating apparel, from working with the pattern to cutting or sewing together parts of a garment through the final stages of finishing or inspecting the item.
- *Wholesale buyers* purchase merchandise directly from manufacturers and resell it to retail firms, commercial establishments, and other institutions. Retail buyers purchase goods from wholesalers (and occasionally from manufacturers) for resale to the general public. In either case, buyers must understand their customers' needs and be able to purchase goods

at an appropriate price and in sufficient quantity.

- *Cost estimators* use standard estimating techniques to calculate the cost of a fashion project. They help designers, executives, and product development managers determine how much a project or product will cost to decide if it is economically viable.
- *Fashion coordinators* are responsible for producing fashion shows and other promotional vehicles for companies and designers. Some are responsible for a particular department, for example, men's apparel, while others may be responsible for the promotion of the entire apparel and accessories line. The majority of these workers are employed by design firms, retail corporations, and apparel centers. Some fashion coordinators work in the entertainment industry.
- *Fashion designers* adapt or create original designs for clothing. Most designers work for textile, apparel, and pattern manufacturers. Some designers are self-employed and develop a clientele of individual customers or manufacturers. Others work for fashion salons, high-fashion department stores, and specialty shops.
- *Fashion illustrators* use a variety of media (for example, pencil, pen and ink, or computer technology) to create illustrations that appear in print and electronic formats.
- *Fashion model agents* act as liaisons between fashion models and clients. They match models to jobs according to a particular look the client desires. Agents arrange for promising models to work with professional photographers, stylists, and other fashion consultants in order to enhance the models' appearance and develop their style. Agents promote their models to potential clients.
- *Fashion models* display clothing and fashion accessories in fashion shows, apparel catalogs, and retail stores.
- *Fashion photographers* take and develop pictures of people, places, and objects using a variety of cameras and photographic equipment.
- *Fashion stylists* work with photographers to create particular fashion images, using props, backgrounds, accessories, clothing, costumes, linens, and other set elements. Much

Did You Know?

- In 2002, the apparel industry provided approximately 358,000 wage and salary jobs.
- There are approximately 14,000 apparel-manufacturing establishments in all 50 states, and most jobs are with large firms.
- More than 66 percent of all U.S. apparel industry workers are employed at companies of 50 workers or more.
- Production workers make up approximately 70 percent of workers in the apparel industry.

Source: U.S. Department of Labor

of the work exists within the print advertising industry, although stylists are also called to do film and commercial shoots.

- *Fashion writers* express, promote, and interpret fashion ideas and facts in written form. Fashion editors perform a wide range of functions, but their primary responsibility is to ensure that text provided by fashion writers is suitable in content, format, and style for the intended audiences.
- *Graphic designers* create the look and feel of products created by the fashion industry, including advertisements, brands, logos, displays, packaging, labels, and magazine covers and interiors.
- *Knit goods industry workers* set up, operate, and repair the machines that knit various products, such as sweaters, socks, hats, sweatshirts, undergarments, lace, and other garments. The work is distinct from weaving, in that knitting consists of drawing one strand of yarn through the loops of another with needles, while weaving builds fabric by interlocking threads at right angles to each other.
- *Leather tanning and finishing workers* make leather out of hides and skins by cleaning, tanning, currying, and finishing them. The leather they produce later is used to manufacture shoes, belts, luggage, gloves, saddles, and many other products.
- *Makeup artists* prepare actors for performances on stage and before cameras. They work with fashion professionals to design makeup effects for fashion shoots and fashion shows.
- *Marketing personnel* in the fashion industry help determine which products will meet consumers' needs and work with store managers, garment makers, and clothing designers to produce and distribute high-quality products.
- *Merchandise displayers,* sometimes known as *visual merchandisers,* design and install displays of clothing, accessories, and other products to attract customers. They set up these displays in windows and showcases and on the sales floors of retail stores. Display workers who specialize in dressing mannequins are known as *model dressers.* Those who specialize in installing displays in store windows are known as *window dressers* or *window trimmers.*
- *Product development managers* oversee the creation of a product from idea stage (such as a new style of hat) to the finished product. They may supervise fashion designers, production workers, advertising and marketing professionals, and other workers.
- *Retail managers* are responsible for the profitable operation of retail trade establishments. These might include department stores; specialty clothing stores, such as the Gap; and boutiques that sell jewelry, handbags, shoes, and other accessories. Their duties include hiring, training, and supervising other employees, maintaining the physical facilities, managing inventory, monitoring expenditures and receipts, and maintaining good public relations.

- *Retail sales workers* assist customers with purchases by identifying their needs, showing merchandise (such as clothing, earrings, or handbags), receiving payment, recording sales, and wrapping their purchases or arranging for their delivery. They are sometimes called *sales clerks, retail clerks,* or *salespeople.*
- *Shoe industry workers* turn materials such as leather, rubber, fabrics, and plastic into finished shoes, boots, moccasins, sandals, slippers, and other footwear. Most of these workers operate machines.
- *Tailors and dressmakers* cut, sew, mend, and alter clothing. Typically, tailors work only with menswear, such as suits, jackets, and coats, while dressmakers work with women's clothing, including dresses, blouses, suits, evening wear, wedding and bridesmaids' gowns, and sportswear. Tailors and dressmakers are employed in dressmaking and custom-tailor shops, department stores, and garment factories; others are self-employed.
- *Textile manufacturing workers* prepare natural and synthetic fibers for spinning into yarn and manufacture yarn into textile products that are used in clothing, in household goods, and for many industrial purposes. Among the processes that these workers perform are cleaning, carding, combing, and spinning fibers; weaving, knitting, or bonding yarns and threads into textiles; and dyeing and finishing fabrics.

EMPLOYMENT OPPORTUNITIES

Employment opportunities for young people entering the fashion industry vary widely. There are opportunities for skilled workers in design, manufacturing, advertising, marketing, purchasing, management, model representation, fashion show coordination, publishing, and countless other areas. The largest center of employment for fashion designers, models, buyers, and other workers in the field is New York. Designers are also employed wherever manufacturing plants are located, and thus can find some employment opportunities in all parts of the United States. Models may work for artists, photographers, fashion designers, clothing manufacturers, retail stores, or at fashion shows. Most U.S. employers of models are in New York City, Chicago, Dallas, Detroit, Los Angeles, Miami, San Francisco, Seattle, and Washington, D.C. Employment opportunities for textile manufacturing workers are concentrated in the southeastern states; approximately 57 percent of all workers in this industry are employed in Georgia, North Carolina, and South Carolina. Apparel industry workers are employed in many settings, from multinational corporations such as Levi Strauss to small companies with few employees. Production jobs are concentrated in Alabama, California, Georgia, New Jersey, New York, North Carolina, Pennsylvania, Tennessee, and Texas, though small clothing manufacturers are located in many parts of the country.

INDUSTRY OUTLOOK

Fashion is constantly in flux, influenced by such factors as international styles as well as the costs of production. In the face of foreign competition, the future of the fashion industry in the United States is unclear. The popularity of imported work from foreign countries has deeply affected the U.S. apparel and textile industries, decreasing U.S. manufacturers' share of the U.S. market. In addition, a provision of the North Atlantic Free Trade Agreement (NAFTA) provides for apparel made in Mexico and Canada to be imported duty-free into the United States. As a result, many U.S. companies have moved their operations across these borders to reduce production costs. Offshore assembly is also a practice that is expected to affect the employment of U.S. workers. In the offshore assembly process, workers from Caribbean countries assemble pieces of fabric that were cut in the United States. The finished product is then imported back into the United States—all at a much lower cost to the manufacturer. As a result of all of these developments, wage and salary employment in the apparel industry is expected to decline 69 percent through 2012—greater than the decrease for nearly any other industry.

Despite this decline, however, improvements such as new spinning and weaving methods, better printing processes, and increased adaptation of computers to manufacturing operations have made the textile and apparel industries more efficient and productive. As new machines and methods are developed and put into place, technical jobs will increase, and lower-skilled, machine-operating jobs will decrease. Because smaller companies cannot afford to make extensive technological changes, some are forced to merge with larger companies. The result is a consolidation of large corporations rather than the many small firms of years ago.

Recent concerns for the environment have led to efforts to reduce the amount of pollution generated by manufacturing plants. For the textile industry, environmental awareness can mean taking steps such as changing ingredients in a chemical used for dyeing, building a water purification system, making a financial contribution for the construction of a municipal waste-treatment facility, or studying the

Fashion Debuts

1700s: Blue jeans
1800s: Left- and right-footed shoes
1896: Buttoned-down collars
1916: Gym shoes
1926: Knee-length hemlines
1930: Designer logos on clothing
1940: Nylon stockings
1946: The bikini
1960s: Paper clothes
1978: Designer jeans
1995: Casual Fridays
2000s: Celebrity-designed clothing

Source: FactMonster.com

recycling of liquids. In the future, there will be an increased demand for people who are trained to protect the natural environment.

The fastest growth in fashion retail is projected for apparel and accessory stores. The market for custom-made clothing is declining as consumers buy more mass-produced apparel. Despite this, the best opportunities for apparel workers are available to the highly skilled. Tailors and dressmakers whose skills are specialized and still necessary in some retail stores, laundries, and dry cleaners, will have better opportunities than most apparel workers.

SECTION 2

Careers

Buyers and Merchandisers

SUMMARY

Definition
Fashion buyers purchase clothing, footwear, and other accessories for retail and wholesale companies. They are usually assigned to a particular specialty such as women's clothing or children's shoes. Fashion merchandisers are responsible for the selection, marketing, and advertising of clothing and accessories for retail and wholesale companies. At many companies, the duties of fashion buyers and merchandisers are interchangeable.

Alternative Job Titles
Merchandising specialists

Salary Range
$24,380 to $42,230 to $79,340+

Educational Requirements
High school diploma

Certification or Licensing
Voluntary

Employment Outlook
More slowly than the average

High School Subjects
Business
Computer science
Economics
Mathematics

Personal Interests
Design
Business
Business management
Economics
Selling/making a deal

INTRODUCTION

"When I was in college," says J. Crew direct merchandiser Joanna Adinolfi, "we talked about Mickey Drexler, while he was at the Gap, in so many of my classes. He is known as the 'merchant prince,' and I had hoped that someday I would be working for a company that he was running. In January 2003, he joined the J. Crew organization and turned this company around so quickly. He truly has lived up to everything that I learned about him while studying his career in college. It has been such an incredible learning experience working under his direction, especially at the first company in my career as a merchant."

WHAT DO BUYERS AND MERCHANDISERS DO?

Fashion buyers purchase clothing for retail stores from designers, manufacturers, or wholesalers. They may specialize in a particular type of apparel such as women's, men's, or children's clothing or accessories such as handbags, footwear, belts, or jewelry. Buyers employed at larger department stores may specialize further within a department, such as women's denim or men's knitwear.

Fashion buyers, armed with a budget set by retail headquarters, develop a buying plan that meets the needs of their store and its customers. Buyers take into account their store's reputation and goals; for example, overly trendy or flashy pieces probably would not sell well at a store that caters to conservative women. Most importantly, buyers listen to the opinions of loyal store customers and which styles they enjoy wearing and clothing lines they look for when shopping. After all, a happy customer signals a job well done.

Fashion merchandisers are responsible for purchasing clothing lines to be sold in retail stores, as well as in wholesale settings. Some merchandisers are assigned to oversee the inventory of one store, though it is not uncommon for merchandisers to be responsible for the inventories of all the stores in a nationwide chain. Merchandisers identify and purchase styles and pieces that they feel will appeal to the customer base. They work with store marketing departments in making choices of when and how such inventory should be purchased and distributed to stores. At times, they work directly with designers to turn ideas into actual fashion pieces. They also maintain contacts with different fashion designers, suppliers, and vendors throughout the world. Travel to different countries is often necessary to inspect designs, fabrics, threads, and other embellishments up close—though more and more of such consultations are done via the Internet.

At some companies, fashion buyers share merchandising duties. In fact, many of the responsibilities of buyers and merchandisers are interchangeable, depending on their place of employment, especially at smaller stores. Both fashion buyers and merchandisers keep up with the current trends by studying market reports, attending endless fashion shows, talking with industry consultants, and finding the latest up-and-coming designers. They have knowledge of different fabrics, textiles, and knitted patterns, and how they look paired with one another. They must also be aware of such details as cost, durability, and cleaning concerns. Merchandisers and buyers, depending on their area of specialty, work with multiple seasonal deadlines. Turnaround time is often lengthy—it takes time to design, sew, and finish clothing pieces—so merchandisers and buyers very often work two or three seasons ahead of what is currently shown in stores.

Once an order is placed, merchandisers and buyers ensure a fair price for the items, and set up a delivery timetable. Upon delivery they check order invoices, and oversee the distribution of merchandise to different stores to confirm adequate stock levels.

Merchandisers and buyers also have a say in how new merchandise is to be displayed in the stores. They often work with advertising and marketing departments in planning decor, signage, lighting, and fixtures such as stands, shelving, and mannequins. They also work alongside stylists in piecing outfits together for display, and adding different accessories to complete a new look. They may work on the creation and updating of store Web sites and print advertising materials. Buyers and merchandisers may also be called upon to explain the season's new themes and colors to store managers and sales staff, giving them better knowledge of the merchandise.

WHAT IS IT LIKE TO BE A BUYER AND MERCHANDISER?

Joanna Adinolfi has worked in merchandising for six years. "I always loved fashion and dressing differently," she says. "My friends in high school all shopped at Gap and other major retailers, but I always shopped at the local boutiques where everything was bought in New York. My friends and sisters always asked me for fashion advice and convinced me that I had an eye for fashion."

Joanna starts her day by checking voicemails and e-mails and her sales reports. "I usually have several different meetings on my calendar every day," she says. "Mondays are always about business and what happened over the weekend, so I spend the first half of my Monday looking at, analyzing, and reacting to the business. Monday afternoons, I meet with my planning team and we discuss sales, markdowns, inventory issues, and what buys need to be placed for the week. I have several standing meetings every week, like fittings with design, tech design, and production. I also have a weekly production meeting where we discuss production issues, delivery slides, and fit approvals. Every Friday, I touch base with my boss to discuss anything and everything, from staff issues to what is going on in the business.

"The entire other side of my job is merchandising the catalog and Internet site. I work very closely with the creative teams to help merchandise the catalog. We have several meetings a week to review styling, approve copy, and catalog features. I work closely with the Internet team to build minisites and approve creative for our Web site. But before all of this happens, I must assort the line each season and allocate units, sales, and space plans for the catalog with my planning team."

To Be a Successful Fashion Buyer and Merchandiser, You Should . . .

- have a great eye for color and fashion
- be creative
- have strong organizational skills
- be an excellent communicator
- be able to work well with all types of people
- have good judgment and confidence in your abilities
- have strong business and marketing skills

Buyers and merchandisers frequently work long or irregular hours. Evening and weekend hours are common, especially during the holiday season, when the retail field is at its busiest. Extra hours may be required to bring records up to date, for example, or to review stock and to become familiar with the store's overall marketing design for the coming season. Travel may also be a regular part of a buyer's job, possibly requiring several days away from home each month. "I travel a few times a year to our distribution center in Virginia," Joanna says. "We also have trunk shows in various cities around the U.S. that I occasionally attend."

DO I HAVE WHAT IT TAKES TO BE A BUYER AND MERCHANDISER?

"To work in this industry," Joanna says, "you must have a great eye for fashion, be creative, organized, be able to articulate thoughts and ideas, be motivated, be able to work with all different types of people, have a great business mind, and always know what your customer wants."

You should also have excellent decision-making skills. Predicting consumer tastes and keeping stores and wholesalers appropriately stocked requires resourcefulness, good judgment, and confidence. You should also have skills in marketing to identify and promote products that will sell. Finally, leadership skills are needed to supervise assistant buyers and merchandisers and deal with manufacturers' representatives and store executives.

HOW DO I BECOME A BUYER?

Education

High School

A high school diploma generally is required for entering this field. Useful high school courses include mathematics,

Employers of Fashion Buyers and Merchandisers

Ann Taylor
(http://www.anntaylor.com)

Bachrach
(http://www.bachrach.com)

Dress Barn
(http://www.dressbarn.com)

GAP, Inc.
(http://www.gapinc.com)

J. Crew
(http://www.jcrew.com)

JCPenney
(http://www.jcpenney.com)

L.L. Bean
(http://www.llbean.com)

Limited Brands
(http://www.limited.com/index.jsp)

Neiman Marcus
(http://www.neimanmarcus.com)

Old Navy
(http://www.oldnavy.com)

Sears, Roebuck and Co.
(http://www.sears.com)

Spiegel
(http://www.spiegel.com)

business, English, and economics. If your high school offers any fashion-related classes, be sure to take them.

Postsecondary Training

A college degree may not be required to be a buyer or merchandiser, but it is becoming increasingly important, especially for advancement. A majority of buyers and merchandisers have attended college, many majoring in fashion merchandising, marketing, advertising, purchasing, or business. Joanna attended the Fashion Institute of Technology in New York City and graduated with a bachelor's degree in fashion merchandising management. Regardless of the major, useful courses in preparation for a career in buying/merchandising include accounting, economics, commercial law, finance, advertising, marketing, and various business classes, such as business communications, business organization and management, and computer applications in business.

Retailing experience is helpful to gain a sense of customer tastes and to witness the supply and demand process. Additional training is available through trade associations, such as the National Association of Purchasing Management, which sponsors conferences, seminars, and workshops.

Certification and Licensing

Certification, although not required, is becoming increasingly important. Various levels of certification are available through the American Purchasing Society and the National Association of Purchasing Management. To earn most certifications you must have work experience, meet education requirements, and pass written and oral exams.

Internships and Volunteerships

As a college student, you will be required to participate in an internship with a retailer or other employer in the fashion industry. Internships typically last from 4 to 12 months. They are excellent methods of learning about the different career options and work settings in the fashion industry.

One way to explore the retailing field is through part-time or summer employment in a store. A good time to look for such work is during the Christmas holiday season. Door-to-door selling is another way to gain retailing experience. Occasionally, experience in a retail store can be found through special high school programs.

WHO WILL HIRE ME?

Buyers and merchandisers work for a wide variety of businesses, both wholesale and retail. Employers range from small stores, where buying and merchandising may be only one function of a manager's job, to multinational corporations, where a buyer or merchandiser may specialize in one type of item. Most buyers and merchandisers find their first job by applying to the personnel office of a retail establishment or wholesaler. Because knowledge of retailing is important, buyers and merchandisers may be required to have work experience in a store.

Large department stores or chains operate executive training programs for college graduates who seek buying, merchandising, and other retail executive positions. A typical program consists of 16 successive weeks of work in a variety of departments. This on-the-job experience is supplemented by formal classroom work that most often is conducted by senior executives and training-department personnel. Following this orientation, trainees are placed in junior management positions for an additional period of supervised experience and training.

WHERE CAN I GO FROM HERE?

Buyers and merchandisers are key employees of the stores or companies that employ them. One way they advance is through increased responsibility, such as more authority to make commitments for merchandise and more complicated buying assignments.

Buyers and merchandisers are sometimes promoted to *merchandise manager,* which requires them to supervise other buyers and merchandisers, help develop the store's purchasing or merchandising policies, and coordinate buying and selling activities with related departments. Some merchandise managers go on to supervise entire divisions—the career path that Joanna would eventually like to take. Other buyers and merchandisers may become vice presidents in charge of purchasing or merchandising or even store presidents. Because buyers and merchandisers learn much about retailing in their job, they are in a position to advance to top executive positions. Some buyers and merchandisers use their knowledge of retailing and the contacts they have developed with suppliers to set up their own businesses.

Related Jobs

- fashion designers
- fashion executives
- marketers
- merchandise displayers
- merchandising distributors
- purchasing agents
- purchasing managers
- retail business owners
- retail managers
- retail sales workers
- sales representatives
- textile manufacturing workers

WHAT ARE THE SALARY RANGES?

How much a buyer or merchandiser earns depends on various factors, including the employer's sales volume. The U.S. Department of Labor reports the median annual income for buyers was $42,230 in 2004. The lowest paid 10 percent of these buyers made less than $24,380 yearly, and at the other end of the pay range, the highest paid 10 percent earned more than

$79,340 annually. Most buyers and merchandisers receive benefits such as vacation, sick leave, life and health insurance, and pension plans.

WHAT IS THE JOB OUTLOOK?

According to the U.S. Department of Labor, employment of buyers and merchandisers in all industries is projected to grow more slowly than the average through 2012. Reasons for this decrease include the large number of business mergers and acquisitions, which results in the blending of buying and merchandising departments and the elimination of redundant jobs. In addition, the use of computers, which increases efficiency, and the trend of some large retail companies to centralize their operations will both contribute to fewer new jobs for buyers and merchandisers. Some job openings will result from the need to hire replacement workers for those who leave the field.

Color Analysts and Image Consultants

SUMMARY

Definition
Color analysts and image consultants use their professional knowledge of color, makeup, wardrobe, grooming, overall appearance, etiquette, and communication skills to help clients excel in a variety of industries.

Alternative Job Titles
None

Salary Range
$15,000 to $40,000 to $100,000+

Educational Requirements
Some postsecondary training

Certification or Licensing
Recommended

Employment Outlook
About as fast as the average

High School Subjects
Business
Mathematics
Psychology
Speech

Personal Interests
Business
Business management
Film and television
Helping people: personal service

In their book *Color Me Beautiful's Looking Your Best,* Mary Spillane and Christine Sherlock cite a study by Albert Mehrabian. He found that the impression we make on others is made up of 55 percent appearance and behavior, 38 percent speech, and only 7 percent the content of what we say. These figures clearly show the importance of presenting yourself well in business, social, and other settings. Color analysts and image consultants play key roles in helping business professionals, as well as people in other industries, such as the fashion and entertainment industries, present themselves in the most flattering and appealing manner.

WHAT DOES A COLOR ANALYST AND IMAGE CONSULTANT DO?

Projecting a positive image through our appearance and behavior helps us gain acceptance from social and business contacts, fit into the workplace, and meet the public. *Color analysts* assess their clients' coloring, including skin tone and hair and eye color, and teach them how to use their most flattering colors in clothing and makeup. *Image consultants* help people present themselves in a professional manner. The majority work with individuals who are hoping to

Advice from a Pro

Marion Gellatly, founder of an image management and consulting firm, offers the following advice to students interested in careers in image consulting:

- Identify the jobs in this field that you are passionate about and have the talent and interest to pursue. For example, I spent many years in the corporate arena before starting Powerful Presence. Therefore, I knew that the corporate arena would be one that would be a natural fit for me and one in which I had expertise, knowledge, and passion to offer to my target market. For example, if you love the environment of retail, you may find it a natural fit to develop a practice focused on personal shopping and/or wardrobe development services. Or if you have a highly artistic and creative talent, you may prefer to develop a personal stylist practice and specialize in the celebrity arena. The opportunities are vast and allow you to select a segment of the business that fits your talent, expertise, and passion.
- If you are building your own practice, you must stay focused on building your business every hour of every day.
- Prior to starting your own practice, you may consider working with a company or retailer that will provide you with learning experiences that you can use in your business.
- Understand and learn what it takes to run a business. Develop a business plan if you will be self-employed. An image consulting practice cannot be run as a hobby if it is to be profitable. And business skills are imperative.

look better, spend their clothing dollars more effectively, and gain more security in making better choices by becoming more educated about clothing and grooming options. People in transition—including those who are making career changes, getting a divorce, seeking a mate, or retiring—are often those who seek image services.

Most color and image consultants are entrepreneurs, meaning that they own and manage their businesses and assume all the risks. They may work with individuals, groups, or both. Many color analysts receive their training regarding color and its use in wardrobe and makeup while on the job. Those who wish to become image consultants take additional training so they can help clients work on their overall appearance and grooming, as well as improve their voices, body language, and etiquette. Consultants may also learn to coach clients on dealing with the public and the media.

Color analysts work in salons, boutiques, day spas, and retail areas, as well as in home-based settings. Many image consultants work out of their homes; others work in traditional office settings. The work is indoors and may involve travel.

WHAT IS IT LIKE TO BE A COLOR ANALYST AND IMAGE CONSULTANT?

Marion Gellatly founded Powerful Presence, a California-based image management training and consulting firm, in 1991. (To learn more about her services, visit http://www.powerful-presence.com/image.htm.) "Powerful Presence's mission," she says, "is to educate and motivate business people to boost their personal power for effective professional presence, etiquette, and communication. The company does this through workshops, seminars, and individual counseling for men and women. We educate and consult with sectors as varied as high tech, finance, government, hospitality, small and large businesses, and professional associations." In addition to her work with Powerful Presence, Marion currently serves as the 2005-2007 president of the Association of Image Consultants International (AICI). AICI is the premier global image organization and represents members in more than 40 countries. Marion is also an executive team member for the Direct Selling Women's Alliance, where she is director of their online Image Center.

Marion's primary responsibilities are to educate and counsel business professionals on the importance of developing, refining, and maintaining an authentic image that helps them achieve their professional goals. Her secondary responsibilities are to provide specific image services for the client (i.e., personal shopping, wardrobe development, color analysis, makeup and hair selections, and communication and business etiquette skills).

DO I HAVE WHAT IT TAKES TO BE A COLOR ANALYST AND IMAGE CONSULTANT?

This is a good field for those who like to work with and help other people and who have an interest in fashion and style. A general flair for art and design would prove useful. Analysts and consultants should be friendly, outgoing, supportive of others, able to offer constructive feedback, and open to change.

Experience in the business world, especially in management and public contact, is essential for corporate consulting. Corporate consultants must be mature, poised, and professional to have credibility when working with clients. Marion says that successful image consultants

To Be a Successful Color Analyst and Image Consultant, You Should...

- be creative
- be detail-oriented and have business acumen
- be self-motivated and ambitious
- have strong communication skills
- be a good listener
- be willing to stay up to date regarding the latest trends in business and other fields
- have entrepreneurial spirit

have integrity, creativity, a passion for learning and educating others, good listening skills, entrepreneurial spirit, and solid business skills (marketing and sales, finance, customer service, and technical).

HOW DO I BECOME A COLOR ANALYST AND IMAGE CONSULTANT?

Education

Marion prepared for this career by spending 20 years in corporate America as a successful businesswoman. "There I learned business acumen, marketing, sales and customer service skills, along with financial budgeting and planning," she says. "I also took a two-year image consulting and fashion merchandising program at a community college. And, I worked in retail for a major, internationally known, high-end retailer, where I was able to apply my knowledge before launching my image consulting firm."

High School

If you are interested in this work, you will benefit from taking classes and being involved in activities that develop your ability to communicate and increase your understanding of visual effects. Helpful classes to take include English, speech, and drama. Activities to consider participating in include drama clubs and debate teams. In drama club you may have the opportunity to help apply makeup, select wardrobes, and learn about the emotional impact appearances can have. Art classes are also helpful to take, especially classes that teach color theory. Since many people in this line of work are entrepreneurs, consider taking any business, bookkeeping, or accounting classes that will give you the skills to run your own business.

Postsecondary Training

There are no formal, standardized training programs for color analysts and image consultants. In general, attending seminars or classes on color, psychology, training methods, business, and communications will be useful training. A degree in liberal arts, with a major in business or education, is a plus for those working at the corporate level.

Certification or Licensing

The Association of Image Consultants International (AICI) provides three levels of certification: First Level Certification, Certified Image Professional, and Certified Image Master. Contact the AICI for more information.

Internships and Volunteerships

If you get to know a color analyst or image consultant personally, you may be able to arrange an informal internship of your own. Some people begin their careers in this field by working as apprentices to other consultants.

Any part-time job working with the public is valuable. You can gain excellent experience from selling clothing or cosmetics in department stores, from working in beauty salons or spas, or from working as a waitperson.

Volunteer work that involves working with people will also help you hone your people skills.

WHO WILL HIRE ME?

For the most part, color analysts and image consultants are self-employed. They run their own consulting businesses, which allows them the freedom to decide what image consulting services they wish to offer. For example, some consultants concentrate on working with corporate clients; other consultants may also advise individuals. Consultants may get the products they sell from one company, or they may offer a range of products and services that provide ways for clients to feel good about themselves. Those in apprenticeships and consultants just entering the field may work for consultants who have already established their businesses.

WHERE CAN I GO FROM HERE?

Workers can advance from color analysts, to image consultants, to trainers by gaining experience and additional education. Salon and department store employees would advance along the path their employers have laid out.

Many who own their own businesses advance by adding new clients, taking advantage of new trends, developing training for future image consultants, and forming alliances with consultants who offer related services. This is par for the course for all self-employed analysts and consultants.

In the next decade, Marion says that she plans to continue her leadership role within the industry and to continue attracting the clients that she enjoys working with, thus creating win-win relationships.

WHAT ARE THE SALARY RANGES?

A color analyst's or image consultant's earnings are determined by the number of hours the consultant works, the

Related Jobs

- buyers
- cosmetologists
- costume designers
- fashion coordinators
- fashion designers
- fashion illustrators
- fashion photographers
- makeup artists
- models
- personal coaches
- personal shoppers
- photo stylists
- photographers
- public relations specialists
- talent agents and scouts

type of clientele, and the consultant's location. Some consultants increase their incomes by offering additional services. Earnings typically start at under $20,000 but can reach $75,000 or more for top performers. Since many color analysts and image consultants own their own businesses, it may also be helpful to consider that some small business owners may earn only about $15,000 a year, while the most successful may make $100,000 or more.

Those who own their own businesses enjoy flexible hours, the ability to control their own time, and opportunity for personal growth and development. Because most consultants are self-employed, they must provide their own insurance and other benefits.

WHAT IS THE JOB OUTLOOK?

The employment of personal appearance workers is expected to grow as fast as the average through 2014, according to the *Occupational Outlook Handbook,* mainly due to increasing population, incomes, and demand for cosmetology services.

The demand for image consultants is growing steadily. Marion says that the Association of Image Consultants International has grown 100 percent in the last five years and is attracting many who desire a career in the field. "The outlook for image consultants is excellent if you are an entrepreneurial person," she says. "The career is easy entry and non-regulated, but to be successful, you must have excellent business skills, creative talent, and be focused and self-motivated."

Fashion Agents

SUMMARY

Definition
An agent is a salesperson who sells artistic talent. Fashion agents act as the representatives for models and other industry professionals, promoting their talent and managing legal contractual business.

Alternative Job Titles
Artists' agents

Salary Range
$26,000 to $45,000 to $100,000+

Educational Requirements
High school diploma

Certification or Licensing
None available

Employment Outlook
About as fast as the average

High School Subjects
Business
Mathematics
Psychology
Speech

Personal Interests
Business
Business management
Current events
Film and television
Helping people: personal service
Law

"We work with hundreds of women with different types of egos," says Emily Bartolome, a fashion model agent in Chicago, Illinois. "It's important to be able to get along with everyone." The fashion world is a highly competitive environment filled with individuals who are, more often than not, used to getting their way. The bottom line: If attitude and diva-esque behavior easily intimidate you, then this job won't be a good fit.

WHAT DOES A FASHION AGENT DO?

While the majority of fashion agents represent models, they also represent fashion designers, illustrators, photographers, and any other professional in the fashion industry whose talents are in demand.

Fashion agents look for clients who have potential for success and then work aggressively to promote their clients to fashion houses or magazines, advertising companies, and other potential employers. Agents work closely with clients to find assignments that will best achieve clients' career goals. When an agent agrees to represent a client, they both sign a contract that specifies the extent of representation, the time period, payment, and other legal considerations.

When agents see a possible match between employer and client, they speak to both and quickly organize meetings, interviews, or auditions, more commonly known as "go-sees," so that employers can meet potential hires and evaluate their work and capabilities. Agents must be persistent and aggressive on behalf of their clients. They spend time on the phone with employers, convincing them of their clients' talents and persuading them to hire clients. There may be one or several interviews, and the agent may coach clients through this process to make sure clients understand what the employer is looking for and adapt their presentations accordingly. When a client achieves success and is in great demand, the agent receives calls and other types of work requests and passes along only those that are appropriate to the interests and goals of the client.

When an employer agrees to hire a client, the fashion agent helps negotiate a contract that outlines salary, benefits, promotional appearances, and other fees, rights, and obligations. Agents have to look out for the best interests of their clients and at the same time satisfy employers in order to establish continuing, long-lasting relationships.

Fashion agents often develop lifelong working relationships with their clients. They act as business associates, advisers, advocates, mentors, teachers, guardians, and confidantes. Because of the complicated nature of these relationships, they can be volatile, so a successful relationship requires trust and respect on both sides, which can only be earned through experience and time. Agents who represent high-profile talent comprise only a small percentage of agency work. Most agents represent lesser-known or locally known talent.

Fashion Model Agencies on the Web

Elite Model Management Corporation
http://www.elitemodel.com/flash.html

Ford Models
http://www.fordmodels.com/main.cfm

Marilyn Agency
http://www.marilynagency.com

mc_ Model Management
(formerly Karin Models)
http://www.mc2mm.com/

ModelScouts
http://www.modelscouts.com

Wilhelmina Models
http://www.wilhelmina.com

The largest agencies are located in New York City and Los Angeles, where the fashion, advertising, and publishing industries are centered. There are modeling and other fashion-related agencies in most large cities, however, and independent agents are established throughout the country.

WHAT IS IT LIKE TO BE A FASHION AGENT?

"Growing up, many of my friends wanted to be models, but I always wondered what it would be like on the other side of the business," says Emily Bartolome, a fashion model agent for Aria, located in Chicago, Illinois.

Bartolome works with about 135 models, some of whom are based in Chicago, others in Los Angeles, Dallas, New York, Miami, and even Canada. Most are between the ages of 16 and 30. While most models work in mainstream fashion (meaning they are typically 5'9" tall and wear size 6), Bartolome does have models doing plus-size work (meaning they wear size 14 and up).

A fashion model agent's job may begin when a client contacts the agency with a possible job assignment. The client, for example, a retail store or an advertising agency, usually will have a specific "look" in mind for the model. The look may include such aspects as the model's hair color, age group, body type, or ethnicity. Once the specifics have been established, the agent refers to his or her "comp board," an area displaying composite cards of models represented by the agency. Composite cards, used much like business cards, are sheets containing photos of the models in a range of poses and have such information as the model's name, measurements, and agency affiliation. Comp boards are often arranged according to such factors as the models' current locations, hair color, or ethnicity. Comp boards make it easier for agents to locate a particular model for a job.

The agent may then send a group of models to the client for an audition, or go-see. There are two types of auditions—a general go-see, which means the client requests a specific look (for example, blondes), and a request go-see, which means the client asks for particular models. If the model is chosen for the job, then he or she is booked, or given the assignment.

Many times an agent is also responsible for arranging a photo shoot for the model as well as transportation if the assignment is out of town. A call sheet is a notice containing all pertinent information regarding the modeling assignment, whether it is a photo shoot, fashion show, or product demonstration. Location and time are listed on the sheet, as well as how the model is expected to look—full makeup and styled hair or clean face and hair. Vouchers, detailing the time worked and hourly wage, are signed by the model and client and returned to the agency for billing purposes. The agency is responsible for billing the client and making certain the model is paid for his or her work. In return, the agency earns a commission from the model, which is typically 15 to 20 percent of the model's total earnings, as well as a commission from the client, which is usually about 20 percent. Some larger agencies will advance a weekly or bi-weekly salary until the model's assignments become more regular or the client has paid for the job. Due to the short-lived careers of most models, agents now wisely provide them with financial planning and advice.

Agents spend a considerable amount of time preparing models for work. Newer models often need help with their portfolio, which provides a list of a model's previous assignments and tearsheets (examples of their work "torn out" of magazines or other publications).

Many times, models need professional help in perfecting their image. Agents may send models to favored stylists for a major change such as a new hairstyle or different hair color. Sometimes, the change may be something subtle such as giving the eyebrows a different arch. Agents may also groom new models in other ways; for example, agents may work to refine the way their models walk or carry themselves.

While agents maintain good working relationships with established clients, they also look for new clients and more assignment possibilities. New retail catalogs are just one source for additional job prospects. "If we come across a new catalog," agent Emily Bartolome says, "we'll call the number, find out where their headquarters are located and where they shoot [the catalog]. Then we send some comp pictures and see if they take a bite."

In addition, fashion model agents are continuously searching for new models. Modeling shows and conventions are held throughout the year all over the United States and abroad. Agents attend such shows to scout for young people, interview and access their modeling potential, and hopefully, sign these promising new talents to modeling contracts. Fashion agents who represent other types of clients in the fashion industry may review a potential client's work (e.g. illustrations, or photographs) via industry Web sites, artist portfolios, or fashion publications.

The environment at a fashion agency is fast-paced and exciting. Most days vary in routine, which can be stressful at times. Agents' workspaces are usually clustered together, where comp boards or folios are easily within reach of an agent. Because of this, privacy is at a minimum.

Most fashion agents work about 40 hours a week, Monday through Friday, in clean, well-lit, indoor offices. Their workspace includes a desk, computer, and telephone. Since a large part of the day is spent on the phone conferring with clients, some agents opt to wear headsets.

Some travel is expected. Modeling conventions and shows, where young people hope to attract agency attention, are scheduled year-round throughout the United States. An agency's presence at these events is important because agents need to keep abreast of new looks and faces coming onto the fashion scene. Agents also need to be aware of trendy social spots and events and frequently socialize after work. Many models have been "discovered" at dance clubs, restaurants, or high-society parties.

While mixing with the fashion elite may seem glamorous and exciting, there is a downside. A small segment of the industry has a reputation for wild living, abusing alcohol and drugs. The fashion agent who wants a long, successful career needs to be levelheaded and able to steer away from such pitfalls.

DO I HAVE WHAT IT TAKES TO BE A FASHION AGENT?

It is most important to be willing to work hard and aggressively pursue opportunities for clients. You should be detail-oriented and have a good head for business; contract work requires meticulous attention to detail. You need a great deal of self-motivation and ambition to develop good contacts in industries that may be difficult to break into. You should be comfortable talking with all kinds of people and be able to develop relationships easily. It helps to be a good general conversationalist in addition to being knowledgeable about your field.

Agents should also be interested in fashion, since they need to stay current on the newest trends of the industry. To do this, agents read a lot during their free time, looking over such magazines as *Vogue* and *Seventeen,* or the trade newspaper *Women's Wear Daily.*

To Be a Successful Fashion Agent, You Should...

- be a good judge of talent
- be willing to work hard and aggressively pursue your clients' interests
- be detail-oriented and have business acumen
- be self-motivated and ambitious
- have strong communication skills
- be interested in fashion
- be willing to stay up to date regarding the latest industry trends

HOW DO I BECOME A FASHION AGENT?

Education

High School

A high school diploma is necessary for work as a fashion agent. If you are interested in pursuing this career, you should concentrate on high school classes such as family and consumer science and art. Take business and mathematics classes since you will be working with contracts and negotiating salaries. English and speech classes will help you develop your communication skills. If your high school offers any sales and marketing courses, be sure to take those. Some high schools offer curriculum targeted to fashion, which may include classes in design, illustration, and sewing. Sign up for these if they're available.

Postsecondary Training

While a college degree is helpful, you don't necessarily need one to get ahead in this industry. Much of the training is learned while on the job. In essence, a model, or designer, or any other type of professional in the fashion industry, is a commodity you are trying to sell; so naturally, any sales experience you have is good. It's important to believe in and be supportive of your client's potential. "If you're not excited about the talent, it's hard to book the model for work," says Emily, who attended Iowa State University and graduated with a bachelor's degree in fashion merchandising. The classes that prepared her for this career included textiles, merchandising and buying, and psychology. On-the-job training may mean working as an assistant, learning to do bookings, keeping track of schedules, and meeting with clients. In this business, your contacts are extremely important. "The fashion world," Emily says, "is very much who you know."

Internships and Volunteerships

Most college fashion programs require students to participate in an internship in the industry. Internships are typically unpaid and last 4 to 12 months. Students receive course credit and excellent opportunities to learn about the field and interact with fashion professionals.

There are a number of ways you can explore this field while you are still in high school; for example, you can hone your selling abilities by getting a part-time or seasonal job at any retail store. Whether you are selling an article of clothing or a model's talent, what's important is your ability to market and sell a product. You can also get actual work experience in the field by applying for any entry-level job at a fashion agency on a part-time or seasonal basis. Even if this means working as the afternoon receptionist, you will have the opportunity to be in the midst of the "action," and more importantly, make contacts for future jobs

WHO WILL HIRE ME?

Talent agencies are located throughout the United States and internationally, though there are established major and minor markets for work. In the United States, the top market is located in New York City, undeniably the fashion capital of the country. Flagship offices of major modeling agencies are located there, such as Ford, Elite, IMG, and Wilhelmina, not to mention top-notch photographers, designers, and advertising agencies. While New York City may offer the best job market and most lucrative bookings, competition for work is intense. Still, many fashion professionals flock to the city in hopes of making it big. And numerous agents also make their way to the city, hoping to represent those promising new talents. Miami, Los Angeles, Chicago, Dallas, and Atlanta are also good markets.

To break into this career, don't be afraid to be aggressive. When agent Emily Bartolome heard that an established modeling agency had come under new ownership, she quickly faxed her resume to their offices. Though she wasn't offered a full-time position right away, she was given the chance to prove her abilities by working as a temp. Two weeks and a successful freelance project later, Emily was hired as an agent.

If permanent, full-time positions are unavailable at a particular agency, you might opt to work as an assistant or in a clerical job while you wait for an opening. Another option is to find out from the agency's human resource department which temporary employment agency they use, get a job there, and request to only be assigned to that specific agency. From there, getting noticed is up to you.

One advantage of going to college is that you will be able to use the school's career services office and network with alumni when you are looking for your first job.

WHERE CAN I GO FROM HERE?

Advancement in this industry can mean representing a larger roster of models or other industry professionals or working with more lucrative client accounts.

Related Jobs

- advertising agents
- buyers
- costume designers
- fashion coordinators
- fashion designers
- fashion illustrators
- fashion photographers
- literary agents
- makeup artists
- models
- photo stylists
- photographers
- sports agents and scouts
- talent agents and scouts

The higher a fashion professional's hourly booking charges, the more the agent's total fee will be. Some agents may choose to move into other areas of the fashion industry and work as a stylist, fashion coordinator, or forecaster of new trends.

Working as an agent is the perfect training ground for sales and management. Experienced and successful agents may opt to open their own agencies representing models, actors, or other forms of talent. Other agents may move outside of the industry and open businesses unrelated to the fashion world.

WHAT ARE THE SALARY RANGES?

Salaries for fashion agents vary depending on such factors as the agent's experience, the size and location of the agency, and the type of professionals they represent. New agents can expect to earn an annual starting salary of approximately $26,000. Those with previous agency experience can earn about $45,000 per year or more. Agents at the top of the industry may earn hundreds of thousands of dollars. Some agencies choose to pay their agents a commission based on fees generated by client/employer bookings. These commissions normally range from 10 to 15 percent of booking totals. Weekly salaries based on commissions may vary according to the amount of booking fees generated and collected.

Agents who work on salary generally receive benefits such as paid vacation and sick time, health insurance, and expense accounts to cover work-related travel costs.

WHAT IS THE JOB OUTLOOK?

Employment in this field should grow about as fast as the average through 2014. New York City will continue to be the hub of the fashion industry in the United States, and many large agencies will stay headquartered there. Agents may find more jobs by representing other professionals in the fashion industry or actors and actresses.

Fashion Coordinators

SUMMARY

Definition
Fashion coordinators are responsible for producing fashion shows and other promotional vehicles for companies and designers.

Alternative Job Titles
None

Salary Range
$25,000 to $37,000 to $100,000+

Educational Requirements
Bachelor's degree

Certification or Licensing
None available

Employment Outlook
About as fast as the average

High School Subjects
Art
Business
Family and consumer science
Mathematics

Personal Interests
Business management
Photography
Selling/making a deal
Travel

"One of the best things about working as a fashion coordinator," says Cathrina Corcuera, a fashion coordinator in New York City, "is the opportunity to meet or be in the same room with fashion 'it' people or icons, as well as work with amazing designers and stylists. For example, I sat behind Anna Wintour [editor-in-chief of *Vogue*] during a fashion show. I've met and been backstage with supermodel icons such as Naomi Campbell and Janice Dickinson." Cathrina says that the main drawback to this career is the number of hours a fashion coordinator must work to ensure that a show is a success. "I often work 18-hour days with no days off in between," she says. "I once worked 20 days straight, averaging 12 hours per day!"

WHAT DOES A FASHION COORDINATOR DO?

Fashion coordinators, whether employed by retail giants, design firms, or shopping centers, are responsible for promoting fashion trends. The main way to promote fashion is through a fashion show. Depending on the size of the company, coordinators may be responsible for a monthly show or for as many as 50 shows or more per year.

There are different types of fashion shows. Vendor or designer shows arrive at the coordinator's office almost pre-packaged. The outfits are already accessorized and are boxed in the order the clothes should be shown. Little preparation is needed to produce this show, aside from booking models and setting up a stage. In addition to choosing which fashions are shown, the designer is also in charge of the commentary and backdrops. Vendor shows typically take only a few days to produce. The designer or design firm owns the rights to these fashion shows. Many vendor-type fashion shows take place within the department's sales floor so the public can shop for the clothes as soon as the show ends.

Trend shows are owned by the retailer and are produced by the fashion coordinator and his or her staff. With these shows, coordinators are responsible for putting together outfits and accessories, choosing the choreography and staging, and most importantly, deciding on the message. Every show sends a particular message, or theme, to the audience; for example, what will be important in fashion for the next season? Leather? Wool? Fur? Trend shows are usually produced two or three times a year and scheduled to coincide with the upcoming season. (Fashions, however, are spotlighted one or two seasons ahead of the calendar year. Spring/summer fashions, for example, will be shown in the fall/winter months.) It often takes a few weeks or a month to put together a trend show.

Trend shows have important public relations value. Oftentimes a sponsor will give additional support to help a retail store in the show's production. Tickets to the show may be sold to the public, and proceeds from the fashion show may be donated to charity. This not only helps promote upcoming fashion lines, but it also highlights the store's interest in supporting worthy causes and provides the sponsor with publicity.

There are several steps to producing a show, regardless of the scale of the production. First, a budget is set. Then models must be cast to fit the type of clothes. Sometimes as many as 300 models are auditioned before the coordinator selects the final 30 or so to work the trend show. Coordinators often use trusted *modeling agents* to find the best men, women, or children. *Stylists* are used to give the models and their clothes a finished look. *Hairdressers, makeup artists,* and *dressers* prepare the models before the show and during outfit changes. *Production workers* are responsible for finding the right music and lighting. The fashion coordinator and assistants are also responsible for the promotion and execution of a fashion show. They send invitations to the public and media and prepare advertising, as well as set up chairs and props and check on other last-minute details.

The fashion coordinator is also responsible for producing fashion shows at other locations. Travel is a large part of this job. Many times, coordinators must go to different departments or boutiques to choose clothing and accessories for a show from various fashion lines. They often travel to other cities and countries to meet with designers, attend shows, or visit other store locations. Meeting with famous designers may be intimidating at first, but as the coordinator gains experience these meetings can become less nerve-racking.

Another important part of a fashion coordinator's job is to help with promotion of a store's fashion lines through television or newspaper and magazine spreads. Oftentimes, local television stations, newspapers, or fashion magazines will request the use of clothing from a store for a particular segment. The TV station may need an outfit for the evening news anchor, for example, or the paper may need an outfit for a model in a travel section. The fashion coordinator pulls the appropriate clothing from the sales floor—be it a business suit or cruise wear—then coordinates the outfits with shoes and other accessories and delivers the chosen items to the TV station, newspaper, or magazine offices. The clothes are later returned to the fashion coordinator and his or her staff, and the store is given credit by the television station or publication in return for their use.

The fashion coordinator's office is part of the marketing side of the fashion industry. Coordinators work alongside *trend forecasters, product developers,* and *planners* in promoting current fashion trends, as well as predicting what the public will desire in fashion for the future.

Most fashion coordinators work 40 hours a week, though it is not unusual to work a lot of overtime, especially when a fashion show is scheduled. Weekend work is expected to meet deadlines.

WHAT IS IT LIKE TO BE A FASHION COORDINATOR?

Cathrina Corcuera begins her day by checking her e-mail and reviewing the day's schedule. She then arranges appointments by sending e-mails or making phone calls to modeling agencies/bookers and designers. "The types of appointments that I must arrange," she says, "include go-sees, in which models from different modeling agencies come to our office and show us their book/portfolio; castings, where, based on our top picks from our go-sees, we work with the designers/clients to cast who will be in the fashion show; and fittings, in which designer clothes are fitted on cast models for the fashion show."

Cathrina says that the show day is very hectic. "I arrive at the venue three hours prior to the show," she says. "I am

To Be a Successful Fashion Coordinator, You Should...

- be willing to put in long hours and work on tight deadlines
- have strong organization skills
- be willing to stay up to date with the latest trends and principle players in the industry
- have an eye for color, design, and what is fashionable
- have strong networking and communication skills

A Short History of the Fashion Coordinator

During the 1970s and 1980s, the fashion industry was revolutionized by the increasing popularity of ready-to-wear fashions. Major designers began to show lines of clothing intended for the average consumer. This move from producing only haute couture to making more affordable—and wearable—clothing allowed fashion to be accessed by the middle class.

The public's interest in fashion was also fueled by the growing importance of fashion in other fields, especially media and entertainment. The careers of stylists and fashion coordinators came from the need to design and advise on the use of fashion in advertising campaigns in print, television, and live formats. Also, the entertainment industry needed fashion experts to help coordinate clothing and accessories for actors, actresses, and musicians. The coordinator working in the entertainment world needs to be aware of the setting (stage, backdrops, lighting) in which the actor, actress, or musician will appear. The fashion coordinator must also use management and office skills to arrange schedules, select locations for shows, keep records, and handle billing.

responsible for keeping track of models' attendance and making sure every hair or makeup artist's chair is filled with a model. For one fashion show, you may be keeping track of up to 30 to 35 models and working with 20 hair and makeup artists. The main goal is to make sure models are ready on time for the show. While the fashion show is going on, I am backstage making sure that the 'run of show' is being executed. This means the girls come out in the correct order and in the correct outfit based on the run of show/program."

DO I HAVE WHAT IT TAKES TO BE A FASHION COORDINATOR?

Fashion coordinators must be hardworking, organized, and well-rounded individuals. They often juggle many tasks simultaneously to meet deadlines or produce a flawless fashion show. Be prepared to mingle with the high-power fashion elite one minute and set up folding chairs the next.

A strong sense of fashion is important. You should have an eye for color, design, and what is fashionable. Fashion sense can be learned, but the interest must be present before it can be nurtured. Cathrina advises new coordinators to "be sure to learn who's who in the industry (the top designers, editors, photographers, fashion stylists, hair and makeup stylist, models, modeling agencies, and production companies) and continually educate yourself about the industry." Fashion coordinators, along with anyone working in the fashion industry, keep current by reading fashion magazines and newspapers and visiting Web sites devoted to fashion. Cathrina also says that successful fashion coordinators need to be well organized, able to solve problems quickly, and have excellent networking skills.

HOW DO I BECOME A FASHION COORDINATOR?

Education

High School

High school classes that are fashion related can help acquaint you with the industry. Some schools, such as the High School of Fashion Industries (http://fashionhighschool.net) in New York City, offer fashion-related courses such as fashion design, illustration, fashion merchandising, and art and art history, along with the more traditional academic classes. Even if your high school does not offer specialized fashion courses, you can still prepare for this work by taking classes such as family and consumer science. Take art classes to learn about color and composition. English and speech classes will help you develop the communication skills essential for this line of work. You may be surprised to find out that a knowledge of math is useful in this field, so don't neglect mathematics courses. You may also want to take business or accounting classes since many fashion coordinators are responsible for accounting and budgeting for fashion shows.

Postsecondary Training

While college education may not be absolutely necessary for every fashion job, in this case, a bachelor's degree plus experience will give you an edge over the candidate working solely on past job skills. Most fashion coordinators have degrees in fashion design and merchandising, marketing, or other business-related courses. Cathrina majored in fashion buying and marketing at the Fashion Institute of Technology in New York City. Computer skills are also important. Many companies rely on computer-aided design software to complete projects.

Internships and Volunteerships

It's imperative to spend time in an internship, preferably with a company you hope to be employed by after graduation. Cathrina interned for several major fashion companies while she was in college. "I worked as a visual merchandiser for Diesel in New York; as a buyer for Selfridges in London, United Kingdom; and as a merchandiser for Calvin Klein in New York," she says. Companies prefer to hire graduates who have relevant work experience. In fact, many companies offer their interns full-time positions. If you are unable to find an internship in the fashion industry, consider internships in the music and entertainment industries. These fields are also important sources of fashion trends. Internships at popular entertainment houses such as MTV or VH1 will give you the opportunity to see the role fashion plays in promoting an image as well as provide you with useful work experience.

Consider volunteering at fashion shows, especially those at the local level.

Related Jobs

- business managers
- buyers
- event planners
- fashion agents
- fashion designers
- fashion photographers
- fashion stylists
- models

Many such productions have smaller budgets, so volunteers are always welcome. No matter what the task, whether helping models with outfit changes, setting up chairs, or passing out brochures, you will get valuable hands-on experience. Take the time to talk to people producing the show and in the show. Ask them about their work and training. You can also make contacts at modeling conventions.

WHO WILL HIRE ME?

Fashion coordinators are employed by retail corporations, fashion companies, and apparel centers. The fashion capitals of New York City, Milan, London, and Los Angeles, of course, will have plenty of employment opportunities, but those who want to enter this business should be ready to face fierce competition. The fashion industry is very tight-knit, and industry contacts are often the best source of jobs. Employment can be found in other areas of the United States, especially large metropolitan areas.

The career of fashion coordinator is not an entry-level position. While being a fashion coordinator may sound like fun, it's a top-level position that is difficult to reach. It takes considerable training and dedication to land a position in this field.

A common career path to take would be to begin as a *stylist*—a person who puts together a particular look for other people through choices in clothing, hair, makeup, and accessories. Some successful fashion coordinators have also climbed the corporate ladder working as assistants to coordinators, fashion directors, or fashion designers. Paying your dues in a lower-level position is important, since many companies like to promote from within the department.

WHERE CAN I GO FROM HERE?

The fashion coordinator position is considered a high rung in the fashion industry ladder. One advancement possibility for a fashion coordinator would be to move deeper into the marketing side of the fashion industry by working as a product developer or fashion forecaster. *Product developers* produce in-house lines of apparel and accessories. *Fashion forecasters,* using a variety of tools, such as surveys, current styles, and market research, try to predict future trends in fashion.

Another way to advance in this career is by transferring to a larger company or design firm, which usually means more responsibilities and a higher salary. With experience and good industry connections, some coordinators may start their own companies. "In five years," says Cathrina, "I hope to excel in this craft and eventually start my own event management and consulting company."

WHAT ARE THE SALARY RANGES?

There are no formal salary surveys available for this particular career. According to industry experts, most salaried stylists should expect to earn from $25,000 to $37,000 annually. Stylists working on a freelance basis can also earn as much, though they are paid only after a project is completed as opposed to weekly or bimonthly. Some successful fashion coordinators, especially those employed by larger corporations or well-known design houses, can earn more than $100,000 a year.

Salaried fashion coordinators and stylists usually receive benefits such as heath insurance, paid vacation and sick time, and retirement plans. Some companies may also offer employee discounts.

WHAT IS THE JOB OUTLOOK?

Employment in this career should be good for the next decade. Many opportunities will occur as a result of the creation of new positions in the field or current employees retiring or leaving the workforce for other reasons. Most jobs in the United States will be available in densely populated areas, especially New York City, Chicago, Los Angeles, and Miami.

As fashion trends change, so too must the way runway shows are presented. Themes reflect the taste of the fashion consumer—flashy styles translate to loud, heavily choreographed shows; understated clothing may call for softer presentations. One style of show, as seen by a popular Chicago fashion show producer, has no spoken commentary. Instead, messages in words and images are shown on the backdrop. More recently, Victoria's Secret produced revolutionary shows that were accessible on the Internet (and were later broadcast on television). By logging on to the company's Web site, the public had a live, front-row view of the latest in lingerie fashions. These new and varied types of shows should provide employment opportunities for the creative and hip fashion coordinator.

Fashion Designers

SUMMARY

Definition
Fashion designers create or adapt original designs for clothing for men, women, and children. Most specialize in one particular type of clothing, such as women's dresses or men's suits, or in accessories such as handbags, hats, or jewelry.

Alternative Job Titles
None

Salary Range
$27,970 to $55,840 to $150,000+

Educational Requirements
Some postsecondary training

Certification or Licensing
None available

Employment Outlook
More slowly than average

High School Subjects
Art
Computer science
Family and consumer science

Personal Interests
Design
Helping people: personal service

Designer Francesca Signorino was recently selected to show her jewelry at the Designer Showcase of Lollapalooza, a popular alternative music and arts festival. "There were live performances by rock bands, and we had a runway fashion show featuring clothing and jewelry designs from a few select artists," she recalls. "It was great because my pieces were used on live models in a large fashion show production. What was really exciting was seeing my name in the advertisements and working with the live models. You really get a great feel for the fashion industry when you are a part of a live runway show! It hasn't brought me much business, but the experience was so fun! Seeing your name in lights and being selected for that event was great! It's those little things that help keep your dream alive!"

WHAT DOES A FASHION DESIGNER DO?

Fashion designers create designs for almost anything that is a part of the costume of men, women, or children. They design both outer and inner garments, hats, purses, shoes, gloves, costume jewelry, scarves, or beachwear. Some specialize in certain types of clothing, such as bridal gowns or sportswear. People in this profession range from the few top haute couture designers who produce

Useful Advice

Fashion design is a highly competitive field. To be successful in this career, you will need to become skilled not only in design, but in countless other areas, such as business and marketing, that will separate you from the pack when it comes to gaining success. The editors of *What Can I Do Now?: Fashion* asked jewelry designer Francesca Signorino for her advice to young people who are interested in pursuing this career:

- Most importantly, go to college and get a degree in some type of business or marketing field. This way you have something to fall back on, plus it will help you start your own business. That is one mistake I made. Sometimes it doesn't matter how talented you may be, but it is very important to know how to run a business—something I am learning the hard way.
- Always ask a lot of questions. Don't ever think a question is stupid; you are only stupid if you don't ask.
- Be open to all kinds of part- and full-time jobs that may not be related to your field. You can learn a lot doing everything from general office jobs to retail work. It will help you gain everything from organizational skills to people skills. Work in retail helps you learn how to deal with both nice and not-so-nice people, and that is invaluable.
- It is good to try and learn the ins and outs of whatever area of fashion you are in. Even if you love jewelry, it's helpful to learn how to knit, sew, and even take up classes in ceramics. You never know where you may get inspiration from or what corner your career may turn . . . you may start out in jewelry and end up being a handbag designer!
- And remember, there may be a lot of people who don't like your work, but you have to know that there will be an equal amount of people who will. Get your designs out there, do what you have to: send free samples, wear it, give it to your friends, market yourself. Join whatever groups and events you can. Be patient and be positive.

one-of-a-kind designs for high-fashion houses, to the thousands of designers who create fashions for mass production and sale to millions of Americans. The majority of fashion designers are followers rather than originators of fashion, adapting high-end styles to meet the desires of the general public. Many fashion designers are self-employed; some work on a freelance basis.

The designer's original idea for a product such as a garment, for example, is usually sketched. After creating the rough sketch, the designer begins to shape the pattern pieces that make the garment. The pieces are drawn to actual size on paper and cut out of a rough material, often muslin. The muslin pieces are sewn together and fitted on a model. The designer makes modifications in the pattern pieces or other features of the rough mock-up to complete the design. From the rough model, sample garments are made in the fabric that the designer intends to use.

Today's designers are greatly assisted by computer software. Computer-aided designing and computer-aided manufacturing allow for thousands of fashion styles and colors to be stored in a computer and accessed at the touch of a button, largely eliminating the long process of gathering fabrics and styling them into samples.

Sample garments are displayed at a "showing," to which *press representatives* and *buyers* are invited to see the latest designs. Major designers may present large runway shows twice a year to leading retailers and the fashion press for potential publicity and sales. Sample garments may then be mass-produced, displayed by *fashion models,* and shipped to stores where they are available for purchase.

In some companies, designers are involved in every step of the production of a selected line, from the original idea to the completed garments. Many designers prefer to supervise their own workrooms. Others work with supervisors to solve problems that arise in the production of the garments.

Most manufacturers produce new styles four times each year: spring and summer; fall and winter; vacation wear; and holiday styles. Designers generally are expected to create between 50 and 150 styles for each showing. Their work calendar differs from the actual time of year. They must be working on spring and summer designs during fall and winter, and on fall and winter clothing during the summer.

Designers work cooperatively with the head of their manufacturing firm. They design a line that is consistent with the ideas of their employers. They also work cooperatively with those who do the actual production of the garments and must be able to estimate the cost of a garment. Some company designers produce designs and oversee a workroom staff, which may consist of a head designer, an assistant designer, and one or more sample makers. Designers in large firms may plan and direct the work of one or more assistant designers, select fabrics and trims, and help determine the pricing of the products they design.

Designers spend time in exploration and research, visiting textile manufacturing and sales establishments to learn about the latest fabrics and their uses and capabilities. They must know about fabric, weave, draping qualities, and strength of materials. A good understanding of textiles and their qualities underlies much of designers' work. They browse through stores to see which fashion items the public is buying and which it is passing on. They visit museums and art galleries to get ideas about color and design. They go to places where people congregate—theaters, sports events, business and professional meetings, and resorts—and meet with marketing and production workers, salespeople, and clients to discover what people are wearing and to discuss ideas and styles.

Designers also keep abreast of changing styles. If the styles are too different from public taste, customers will reject the designs. If, however, they cling to

Finding Inspiration

Designers find inspiration in a variety of ways. Some look to nature, others listen to music, and some may end up jotting down ideas that came to them in a dream! We asked Francesca Signorino and Kathryn Swan to discuss their sources of inspiration:

Francesca Signorino: I love art, and my travels, although they may be infrequent, have inspired me greatly. I am intrigued by different cultures. Also anything Gaudi, Frank Lloyd Wright, antiques, rock gardens, trends, ancient artifacts, energy, and the ever-changing world around us! I am also inspired from the need to accessorize my own wardrobe! Sometimes I need those shoe clips to complete an outfit—hence, a pair of earrings become shoe clips! Or a fun hair clip! I can look at an interesting drawer, pull on a cabinet, and boom . . . a new pendant! You never know. Being creative is a great thing; you always have something unique and different to wear because you were inspired to have a new look. What is the saying, 'necessity is the mother of invention'? Well, I say, 'the need to change an old look into a new look is the mother of invention'!

Kathryn Swan: I draw my inspiration from a variety of sources, but in particular I'm influenced by literature, art, travel, and trips to the hardware store, as well as by the fabric itself. I also find inspiration in studying the history of fashion and culture and their reciprocal influence on each other. On a practical level, I greatly enjoy the challenge of creating new functional shapes—handbags that have clean lines but are infused with unique innovative touches to provide interest and a focal point.

styles that have been successful in the past, they may find that the taste of buyers has changed dramatically. In either case, it could be equally disastrous for their employers.

There are many opportunities for specialization in fashion designing. The most common specialties are particular types of garments such as resort wear, bridal wear, or sportswear. Other designers specialize in accessories, such as handbags or jewelry. Kathryn Swan, a designer of eclectic handbags, is the owner of Felix & Agatha in Chicago, Illinois. (To view her designs, visit http://www.felixandagatha.com.) "I enjoy creating unusual, yet functional, shapes for my bags with a style that I call 'cheeky sophistication'—generally clean lines with girly touches, which transition well for being either day or evening bags." Kathryn has worked as a full-time designer for nearly two years, but has been designing for approximately 15 years on her own. "Several years ago," she says, "I branched into handbag design from apparel and decided that was the direction I wanted to move for starting my own company."

Another interesting specialty in fashion designing is theatrical design, a relatively limited field but challenging to those who are interested in combining an interest in theater with a talent for clothing design.

WHAT IS IT LIKE TO BE A FASHION DESIGNER?

Francesca Signorino is the owner of Francesca Signorino Designs in Lincolnshire, Illinois. She has designed jewelry and worked in the fashion industry for 13 years. (To view her designs, visit http://www.signorinodesigns.com.) "The pros of this business are that you can be as creative as you want," she explains, "and you are your own boss. It is so great knowing that you designed something that people want and like. There is a lot of self-reward, and you get to meet a lot of interesting people."

Francesca designs both fine jewelry and fashion jewelry. "My primary focus right now is on fashion jewelry," she says. "My pieces are made of unusual semi-precious beads in combination with sterling silver. My fine jewelry consists of 14kt yellow gold and white gold, sometimes accented with diamonds."

Francesca spends anywhere from 3 to 12 hours a day creating jewelry. "I rarely sketch my pieces first," she says. "I usually look at my beads and my shapes of metal and start to play with them and configure them in different ways to see how they will hang, etc., and then assemble them. I am not at the stage to hire people, so I make the jewelry myself."

In addition to designing her jewelry, Francesca must also make time for other tasks that help her to run and grow her business. "I try to set aside one day for designing, one day for paperwork, one day for research, and so on," she says. "Sometimes it takes longer if I have let things pile up. However, when you are a creative thinker, it may be difficult to do paperwork on a day you are feeling creative. So I change my plans and design."

In addition, Francesca must constantly focus on promoting her designs and business. "I try to research the industry and see what is selling," she explains. "I am constantly reading both fashion and trade magazines. I developed a Web site and try to do as much advertising as possible. I also try to have home-based parties. That involves printing up business cards, invitations, displays (to show the jewelry on), packaging, labels, receipts, and more. The more your name is out there, the better. Advertising can be very costly (when you are just starting out, it can be impossible), so word of mouth is always great." Francesca also sends out free samples to magazine editors in hopes of getting a write-up in their magazine. "You can't get discouraged because you will get a lot of rejection," she advises. "You have to keep on trying!"

Most designers work a 40-hour week, but they may have to work more during rush periods. Styles previewed for one season require a great amount of work during the weeks and months before a show. The work pace is usually hectic as pressure builds before collection showings. Self-employed designers have more flexible schedules. Francesca works anywhere from 30 to 60 hours a week. "Some days you just are not as motivated as others,"

To Be a Successful Fashion Designer, You Should...

- have strong artistic ability
- be able to conceptualize in two and three dimensions
- have the ability to handle deadline pressure
- have business acumen
- be able to accept constructive criticism regarding your designs

she says, "and some days you need to make up for the days you were not inspired." Kathryn Swan typically works 50 or more hours per week, but she says that this can vary based on the project.

Fashion design is competitive and stressful, but often exciting and glamorous. Many designers work in cluttered and noisy surroundings. Their work environment may consist of a large room with long tables for cutting out patterns or garments or working with other materials. There may be only one or two other people working in the room, or there may be several other workers. Many designers travel a great deal for showings and conferences. They may spend time in stores or shops looking at clothing that has been manufactured by competitors. As she builds her line of jewelry, Francesca Signorino believes that she will eventually travel to trade shows to show her products. Kathryn Swan travels on occasion, "the first reason," she explains, "being to meet with boutiques regarding sales and, secondly, traveling for inspiration for new designs. Thus far, my travels to meet with boutiques have been all domestic, but I also travel internationally to take in and experience other fashions, museums, [and] art."

DO I HAVE WHAT IT TAKES TO BE A FASHION DESIGNER?

Prospective fashion designers must be artistic and imaginative, with a flair for color and clothing coordination. They will need a working knowledge of clothing or accessory construction and an eye for trends. They must possess technical aptitudes, problem-solving skills, and the ability to conceptualize in two and three dimensions. Personal qualifications include self-motivation, team spirit, and the ability to handle pressure, deadlines, and long hours. This career also demands energy and a good head for business.

HOW DO I BECOME A FASHION DESIGNER?

Education

Francesca Signorino began her career in design not working with jewelry, but with large-scale sculpture. "I studied welding while taking classes in accessory and fashion design," she recalls. "It just made sense to marry the two. I have always loved gems and jewelry, and I have always loved art. I took classes that involved shoemaking, papermaking, knitwear design, glassblowing, and designing clothing. I really loved it all, but I needed to focus on one thing. Being that I have a real passion for interiors, architecture, and Asian gardens—I tried to combine the nature of stones and incorporated it with the architecture of my pieces."

Kathryn Swan obtained her training as a fashion designer from mostly indirect sources. "My training began when I was taught to sew around the age of five," she explains. "Learning to sew and seeing my mother creating clothing for me and my dolls as a young girl started my love of experimenting with fabric and caused me to start designing on my own while in high school. While I have not had formal training in fashion, I have honed my skills over the years on my own. Additionally, I learned a great deal about business in general from my years working at a corporate real estate firm after graduating from college. Though the fields are completely different, a lot of the skills and knowledge I gleaned while there have helped me in knowing how to run my current business."

High School

A high school diploma is needed to work as a fashion designer and should include courses that prepare you for more specialized training after graduation. Art, family and consumer sciences, mathematics, and chemistry all should be included.

Postsecondary Training

An aspiring designer with a fashion background that includes marketing and other business skills will be favored by employers over a talented person with no knowledge of business procedures. A college degree is recommended, although not required. Graduation from a fashion design school is highly desirable. Employers seek designers who have taken courses in mathematics, business, design, sketching, art history, costume history, literature, patternmaking, clothing construction, and textiles.

Some colleges offer a four-year degree in fine arts with a major in fashion design. Many reputable schools of fashion design offer a two- or three-year program that offers a diploma or certificate. Francesca Signorino earned a bachelor of fine arts degree from the School of the Art Institute of Chicago and then went on to obtain a Graduate Gemologist degree from the Gemological Institute of America in Santa Monica, California. "After college," she says, "I began doing apprentice work for a master goldsmith. I did that for about four years. It involved a lot of hard work, long hours, and low pay. However, the education was invaluable. I learned how to do repairs, solder properly, cast, polish, draw down my own wire, and much more than I could have learned from local park-district classes. I then went on to work in the jewelry appraisal end of the business, and from there I worked with high-end jewelry in a retail setting. Before really launching my business, I also worked as an assistant buyer for a chain of jewelry stores. It is really a must to know all avenues of this industry. There are so many different areas that you really need to master before moving on to just designing."

If you are interested in fashion, you should also take computer-aided design courses, as computers are increasingly being used by designers to better visualize a final product, create prototypes, and reduce design production time and cost. Companies are looking for more than design skills; many require extensive knowledge and experience with software programs used to produce technical drawings.

Internships and Volunteerships

Most postsecondary fashion design programs include an internship segment where you will be required to work at fashion design houses, with fashion designers, or in other fashion-related settings that will help you learn more about the career. You might also consider volunteering at a design house or with a freelance designer to gain a valuable introduction to the field.

WHO WILL HIRE ME?

Few people begin their careers as fashion designers. Well-trained college graduates often begin as *assistant designers.* Assistants must prove their ability before being entrusted with the responsibility of the designer's job. Many young people find that assistant designer jobs are difficult to locate, so they accept beginning jobs in the workroom where they spend time cutting or constructing garments or working with other materials.

Fashion design school graduates may receive placement information from their school or career services offices. Approaching stores and manufacturers directly is another way to secure a beginning position. You will be more successful, though, if you have contacts in the industry through previous summer or part-time work.

Many clothing fashion designers find employment with large fashion houses such as Liz Claiborne or Jones New York. Some large manufacturers produce a secondary line of lower-priced designer clothing—Donna Karan's DKNY and Giorgio Armani's Emporio, for example. In the United States, New York City, San Francisco, and Los Angeles are major fashion centers and positions may be found in both large and small companies. Work may also be found in Chicago and other cities, although not as many jobs are available in these locations.

A few fashion designers work for high-fashion firms, but these positions are difficult to come by and competition is very strong. An aspiring designer may have more options in specialized areas of fashion such as sportswear, sleepwear, children's clothing, or accessories.

Other areas for aspiring fashion designers to explore are home fashions such as bed and bath linens, draperies, and rugs or carpeting. Positions can also be found with pattern manufacturers. Some fashion designers work on a freelance basis, contracting with manufacturers or individuals.

An easy way to learn about manufacturers is to visit a department or specialty store and examine labels and tags on merchandise of interest. In addition to major department stores, retailers such as Target carry a variety of manufacturers' lines.

WHERE CAN I GO FROM HERE?

Advancement in fashion designing varies a great deal. There is much moving from firm to firm, and vacancies occur frequently. Aspiring designers should create, collect, and continuously update their portfolios of designs and look for opportunities to show their work to employers. Beginners may work as cutting assistants or assistant designers. From these entry-level positions, the fashion designer's career path may lead to positions as an assistant technical designer, pattern company designer, designer, and head designer. Those who grow with a company may design less and take on more operational responsibilities.

Designers may choose to move into a business or merchandising position where they direct lines, set prices, supervise production, and work directly with buyers. After years of work, top designers may become partners in the design or apparel firms for which they work. Others may open their own retail stores. At this time, Francesca Signorino is not interested in opening her own store, but is keeping her options open. "Right now," she says, "I would love to have my Web-based business take off, and I would be very happy to have some larger department stores carrying my line. I wouldn't mind some celebrities wearing my pieces, too!"

"After working on solidifying my current line of handbags, I would like to move into shoe design," Kathryn Swan says. "I have found that accessory design is a favorite area of mine and would like to explore that further."

Related Jobs

- apparel industry workers
- costume designers
- fashion agents
- fashion coordinators
- fashion illustrators
- fashion model agents
- fashion photographers
- fashion stylists
- fashion writers and editors
- jewelers and jewelry repairers
- models
- shoe industry workers
- tailors and dressmakers

WHAT ARE THE SALARY RANGES?

Fashion designers earned an average annual salary of $55,840 in 2004, according to the U.S. Department of Labor. The lowest paid 10 percent earned less than $27,970; the highest paid 10 percent earned more than $112,840. A few highly skilled and well-known designers in top firms have annual incomes of more than $150,000. Top fashion designers who have successful lines of clothing can earn bonuses that bring their annual incomes into the millions. As designers become well known, they are usually offered a share of the ownership of the company for which they design. Their ownership percentage increases with their reputation.

Fashion designers who are self-employed do not receive a steady paycheck and have to pay for their own health insurance and other benefits typically provided by a full-time employer. "You really need to be self-motivated to work in this career," Francesca Signorino advises. "You do not see an income for a long time, and you cannot get discouraged. I sometimes have to take on jobs temporarily to keep money coming in, so it can be hard juggling both. You must trust yourself as a designer, and we usually can be our own worst critics. You need to put in a lot of long hours, and there are times when you don't feel creative . . . but when you do feel creative, there is no stopping."

WHAT IS THE JOB OUTLOOK?

Designers are key people in the garment industry, yet relatively few of them are needed to make employment possible for thousands of people in other apparel occupations. It is estimated that there are approximately 15,000 fashion designers in the United States, which represents less than 1 percent of the garment industry. Some designers work only for the high-priced custom trade, some for the mass market, and some on exclusive designs that will be made for only one person. Many designers are employed by manufacturers of paper patterns.

Good designers will always be needed, although not in great numbers. However, increasing populations and growing personal incomes are expected to spur the demand for fashion designers. According to the *Occupational Outlook Handbook,* employment of designers is expected to grow more slowly than the average for all occupations through 2014.

Some fashion designers enjoy high pay and prestige. Those at the top of their profession rarely leave their positions. Therefore, opportunities for newcomers are limited. There always will be more people hoping to break into the field than there are available jobs. Experience working with computer-aided design programs is increasingly important to employers and can help to distinguish a qualified job candidate from the rest of his or her competition. Employment prospects may be better in specialized areas, such as children's clothing. Additionally, openings are more readily available for assistant designers.

Fashion Illustrators

SUMMARY

Definition
Illustrators prepare drawings for advertisements, magazines, books, newspapers, packaging, Web sites, computer programs, and other formats. Fashion illustrators specialize in distinctive illustrations of the latest women's and men's fashions.

Alternative Job Titles
None

Salary Range
$17,390 to $38,060 to $68,860+

Educational Requirements
Some postsecondary training

Certification or Licensing
None available

Employment Outlook
About as fast as the average

High School Subjects
Anatomy and physiology
Art
Computer science

Personal Interests
Design
Drawing

One of the great things about the fashion illustrator career is the variety of projects on which to work. Three of Renie Hanna's recent assignments illustrate the opportunities available to talented professionals in the field. "For L'Oreal's MATRIX hair color product," she says, "I drew headshots of models' hair . . . golds and reds and streaks of highlights. Loreal then took these illustrations to Paris and turned them into animations. I also recently worked with the U.S. Armed Services to create uniforms for their sergeants and officers. And I also drew the uniforms for the staff of three hotels in Las Vegas. A company asked me to create about 100 illustrations for these uniforms in about two to three weeks. It was a real rush project, but I got it done, and it turned out perfectly. It is important to be able to meet tight deadlines."

WHAT DOES A FASHION ILLUSTRATOR DO?

Fashion illustrators use a variety of media to create illustrations that are used to advertise new fashions (such as clothing, cosmetics, shoes, accessories, and beauty products), promote models, and popularize certain designers. Their illustrations might appear in newspapers such as *Women's Wear Daily,* magazines such as *Glamour, Redbook,* and *Vogue,* and in online and print catalogs.

Fashion Illustration Programs

Art Center College of Design
http://www.artcenter.edu/accd/programs/undergraduate/illustration.jsp

Art Institute of Ft. Lauderdale
http://www.artinstitutes.edu/fortlauderdale/

Fashion Institute of Technology
http://www.fitnyc.edu/aspx/Content.aspx?menu=Future:SchoolsAndPrograms:ArtAndDesign:Illustration

Fashion-Schools.org
http://www.fashion-schools.org

Maryland Institute of Art
http://www.mica.edu/PROGRAMS/bfa/illustration/index.cfm?id=360

Parsons School of Design
http://www.parsons.edu/departments/department.aspx?dID=75&sdID=99&pType=1

Fashion illustrators work with fashion designers, editors, and models. They make sketches from designers' notes or they may sketch live models during runway shows or other fashion presentations. They may use pencils, pen and ink, charcoal, paint, airbrush, computer technology, or a combination of media.

Although fashion illustrators typically have well-lit, organized workspaces, with room to accommodate their tools, they are also in a fast-paced, deadline-driven environment. They may be required to attend fashion shows and other industry events. Illustrators may often need to put in long or irregular hours to complete an assignment to a client's satisfaction. Freelance illustrators have the added pressure of continually seeking new clients and uncertain incomes.

WHAT IS IT LIKE TO BE A FASHION ILLUSTRATOR?

Renie Hanna is a freelance fashion illustrator and designer in New York City. Her work has appeared in many publications including *Martha Stewart Weddings, BrandWeek, Women's Wear Daily,* and the *New York Times.* Her clients include Nautica, Donna Karan, Scassi, Oleg Cassini, Joseph Abboud, Evan Picone, Adolfo, Charles Lima Chang, Liz Claiborne, and Tiffany's. (Visit http://www.renie.com to view samples of her work.) "I feel very fortunate to have this job," she says. "I get the opportunity to work with very interesting clients. I also love the actual drawing. Right now, I'm working on all brand new material. I'm working on a new Web site. I am adding some very special and dynamic features to my site with some of my new current material and also my classic and edgy illustrations."

Renie works out of a studio that is located in her apartment. She spends much of her day interacting with clients via e-mail, phone, and in person. "We talk about the projects on the phone, they FedEx or messenger me the materials that I need, and I get to work," she says. "They might send me an unfinished sketch that they have drawn, a photograph, or a flat, which is a construction of the garment and its dimensions drawn out on paper without the body of a model. I find a model's pose in a magazine (I have millions of magazines with all types of poses) or online, and I draw the clothing onto the model. The designer or the company that you are working with also usually sends swatches that have all the colors they want in the illustration. I have to match up the color of the swatch with my markers—I have probably 1,000 different colored markers—that I put down on the paper when I draw my illustration."

Renie says that successful fashion illustrations have "a lot of color, a lot of movement, a lot of energy, and a confident attitude. Every illustrator has to come up with his or her own style because you will become known and recommended for your style. Additionally, it is important to make sure that the illustration helps convey a message about the client's clothing, because ultimately you are not just illustrating but helping to sell the client's clothing in the best way."

To Be a Successful Fashion Illustrator, You Should...

- be creative
- have artistic talent and skill
- be flexible regarding assignments and project deadlines
- love the world of fashion and enjoy expressing style through images
- have good business acumen, especially if you own your own business
- be willing to accept constructive criticism regarding your work
- have confidence in your abilities and artistic vision

DO I HAVE WHAT IT TAKES TO BE A FASHION ILLUSTRATOR?

Fashion illustrators must be creative, and, of course, demonstrate artistic talent and skill. They also need to be flexible since the scope and deadlines of a project may change at the whim of a designer. Because their art is commercial in nature, illustrators must be willing to accommodate their employers' desires if they are to build a broad clientele and earn a decent living. They must be able to take suggestions and rejections gracefully. And, naturally, illustrators must have a love of fashion and enjoy expressing style through images.

Education

High School

Creative talent is more important in this field than education; however, there are academic programs in illustration at most colleges and universities. If you are considering going on to a formal program, be sure to take plenty of art classes while in high school. Elective classes in illustration, ceramics, painting, or photography are common courses offered at many high schools. If you plan to start your own business, be sure to take business, accounting, and mathematics classes. And take computer classes because knowledge of computer drawing software and other technology is becoming increasingly important to fashion illustrators. Finally, take as many courses in anatomy and physiology as possible. "Students should definitely take anatomy," Renie advises. "It is very, very important to learn the human body and get its proportions right when you are drawing."

Postsecondary Training

To find a salaried position as a fashion illustrator, you should have at least a high school diploma and preferably an associate or bachelor's degree in fashion illustration, commercial art, or fine art. Renie attended several postsecondary institutions to hone her artistic skills, including the Fashion Institute of Technology in New York City; the Parsons School of Design in New York City and Paris, France; the Pratt Institute in New York City; and the John Murry School of Art in New York. She also participated in private study with renowned illustrator Antonio Lopez. "I studied with him in the Dominican Republic years ago," Renie says. "I would say he was my mentor. I really enjoyed studying with him, and I admired all of his work. He invited me for lunch at his villa. He looked at my portfolio and he told me that I had a great flair for fashion."

Illustration studies will include drawing, painting, layout, color, and design. Whether you are looking for full-time employment or freelance assignments, you will need an organized collection of samples of your best work, which is called a portfolio. Employers are especially interested in work that has been published or printed. One advantage of pursuing postsecondary education is that it gives you an opportunity to build your portfolio. Fashion illustrators should also study clothing construction, cosmetology, fashion design, and anatomy and physiology. And they should keep up with the latest fashion and illustration trends by reading fashion magazines.

Internships and Volunteerships

If you pursue training in illustration or art at the postsecondary level, you will be required to participate in an internship. Internships are typically unpaid and last

Typical Illustration Courses

- The Illustrator's Heritage
- Book Illustration
- Visual Self-Expression
- Materials and Techniques
- Advanced Drawing
- Photo Reference and Digital Editing
- Digital Sketching and Comping
- Film and Computer Animation
- Advanced Computer Illustration
- Advanced Quark
- Color Rendering/Advanced Media
- Digital Special Effects and Photo Retouching
- Illustration Workshop

Source: Fashion Institute of Technology

anywhere from 4 to 12 months. As an intern, you might work as an illustrator's assistant at fashion firms (called *houses*), or in another setting.

If you are still a student, you might consider volunteering or finding part-time employment with a fashion illustrator or a fashion house. If you can't find such an opportunity, try getting a job at a clothing store. This will give you experience working with people and clothes, and you might even be able to suggest fashion advice to customers.

Related Jobs

- art directors
- art teachers
- cartoonists
- children's book illustrators
- fashion designers
- fashion photographers
- graphic designers
- medical illustrators
- mixed-media artists
- painters
- police artists
- printmakers
- scientific illustrators

WHO WILL HIRE ME?

More than 50 percent of all visual artists (including illustrators) are self-employed. Others work for large retailers, magazines, newspapers, design or advertising firms, and fashion houses.

Graduates of illustration programs should develop a portfolio of their work to show to prospective employers or clients. Most schools offer career counseling and job placement assistance to their graduates. Job ads and employment agencies are also potential sources for locating work.

WHERE CAN I GO FROM HERE?

Salaried fashion illustrators advance by being assigned more challenging and unusual work or taking on a supervisory position. Others move on to work for more prestigious companies. Freelance fashion illustrators advance by developing a reputation for creativity and the high quality of their work. This allows them to charge more for their services and be more selective about the assignments they take. Fashion illustrators can also go into teaching at colleges and universities.

"I would like to eventually spend more time designing and have my own design line," Renie says, "and/or work as the illustrator for every top designer in the world. I also am a gourmet cook, and I'd like to do a fashion cookbook and illustrate it."

WHAT ARE THE SALARY RANGES?

According to the U.S. Department of Labor, salaried fine artists, including illustrators, had median yearly incomes of approximately $38,060 in 2004. Salaries ranged from less than $17,390 to

$68,860 or more annually. Fine artists who were employed in advertising and related services had mean annual earnings of $44,960 in 2004. Some illustrators can earn several thousand dollars for a single illustration.

Illustrators generally receive good benefits, including health and life insurance, pension plans, and vacation, sick, and holiday pay. Those who work as freelancers do not receive benefits such as health insurance, or paid sick or vacation days. Additionally, freelance work is often uncertain because of the fluctuation in pay rates and steadiness of work. "When you're working, it's great," Renie says. "It's a lot of fun, I enjoy it, and its very satisfying. But the downside of this job is that like any other commissioned artist, you never know when your next job is going to be. You may get a lot of work all at once, and then nothing."

WHAT IS THE JOB OUTLOOK?

Employment of visual artists is expected to grow about as fast as the average for all occupations through 2014, according to the *Occupational Outlook Handbook.* The outlook for careers in fashion illustration is dependent on the health of the magazine publishing, advertising, and fashion industries. Growth of advertising and public relations agencies will provide new jobs. The popularity of American fashion in other parts of the world will also create a demand for fashion illustrators to provide the artwork needed to sell to a global market.

Fashion Photographers

SUMMARY

Definition
Fashion photographers take photographs that help advertise new fashions, promote models, and popularize certain designers; they work in both print and electric formats.

Alternative Job Titles
None

Salary Range
$15,000 to $37,370 to $100,000+

Educational Requirements
Some postsecondary training

Certification or Licensing
None available

Employment Outlook
About as fast as the average

High School Subjects
Art
Business
Computer science

Personal Interests
Design
Photography

Asked to name the most interesting aspect of his career, Eric Stephenson, a fashion photographer in Denver, Colorado, has trouble choosing just one. "It's not so much a single isolated event," he says, "but the wonderful creative energy that develops on the best shoots. Shoots can feel truly magical, and when I am able to translate that magic to film in images that are new, exciting, and which evoke strong emotions . . . that is a wonderful feeling. That is why I am a photographer."

WHAT DOES A FASHION PHOTOGRAPHER DO?

Fashion photographers work in the exciting world of fashion. Their skills are focused specifically on styles of clothing and personal image. They take and develop pictures of people, places, and objects while using a variety of cameras and photographic equipment.

Fashion photography is a specialized form of photography that requires working on a team with designers, editors, illustrators, models, hair stylists, photo stylists, and makeup artists. Shooting takes place in a studio or on location, indoors and outdoors. Photographers use cameras, film, filters, lenses, lighting equipment, props, and sets. Their first priority is to satisfy the client's requirements. Some photographers develop a unique artistic style that earns them recognition and higher earnings.

Fashion photographers can work in any of several different areas of the fashion field. They provide artwork to accompany editorial pieces in magazines such as *Glamour, Marie Claire,* and *Vogue* and newspapers such as *Women's Wear Daily.* The advertising industry is probably the largest employer of fashion photographers who create the pictures that sell clothing, cosmetics, shoes, accessories, and beauty products. Catalog companies employ photographers to provide images that will sell their merchandise through print or online publications.

Photographers may work as freelancers, handling all the business aspects that go along with being self-employed. Such responsibilities include keeping track of expenses, billing clients promptly and appropriately, and keeping their businesses going by lining up new jobs for when a current project ends. Establishing oneself in the field can take years, and this is also a stressful process. On the positive side, fashion photographers are able to enjoy working in creative environments where visual images are highly valued.

Because the fashion world is extremely competitive and fast-paced, fashion photographers tend to work long hours under the pressure of deadlines and demanding personalities.

Photographers' working conditions vary based on the job and the employer. For some jobs they will work in a comfortable studio, while for others they may be on location, working on a dark street, or in the snow, or at a crowded fashion show.

WHAT IS IT LIKE TO BE A FASHION PHOTOGRAPHER?

Eric Stephenson is the owner of Eric Stephenson Photography in Denver, Colorado. He has been a professional photographer for the past 15 years, but he has done the bulk of his work in fashion photography in the past five years. "Like most photographers outside of New York, Los Angeles, or a few other select areas, fashion photography does not comprise all of my business, but rather a portion of it," he explains. (Visit http://www.stephensonphoto.com to view samples of Eric's work.)

Eric first picked up a camera when he was about 10 years old. By the age of 16, he was working as a photographer for his high school paper shooting a mixture of sports and street photography. "Although I studied Spanish in college," he says, "photography became an evermore important part of my life. I initially was much more interested in showing my work in galleries, but practical concerns eventually led me to pursue a career in commercial photography."

Like most photographers, Eric's work days do not follow a set routine. "For large shoots, the work begins days or even weeks or months prior to the actual shoot," he says. "There are usually numerous telephone conversations, e-mails, and such to determine the client's needs, determine the logistics, and coordinate the schedules of all the key players: clients, art directors, models, stylists, assistants, etc. On the day or days prior to the shoot I check and organize all the equipment, clean camera sensors, reformat memory cards, and perform related tasks."

On the day of the shoot Eric generally arrives several hours prior to the shoot to set up the lighting and backgrounds, test exposures, check color temperature settings, and prepare for contingencies. "By the time the models arrive everything is in place for the first shots," he says. "I have the backgrounds and any props in place, have produced test shots, and determined the initial camera angles and compositions that I wish to use. Additional equipment and set material is ready nearby for the variations that I may wish to employ after the initial shots. I also make sure we have areas set up for the stylists, clients, and art directors, as well as food and beverages to keep everyone comfortable and anything else that I think we will need. If it is an outdoor or location shoot I will have already scouted out a variety of locations as changing weather conditions (angle of the sun, clouds, rain, wind, etc.) and numerous other variables can make a specific location less desirable at the moment of the shoot. I usually begin the shoot with preconceived ideas, but then my approach evolves throughout the actual shoot as it is influenced by the clothing styles and personalities involved."

Eric says that the bulk of his work these days is digital rather than film based—which has dramatically changed his workflow. "It used to be that the transparency film would be taken to a commercial lab following the shoot, edited the next day on a light table in one to four hours, and that was the end of it for the photographer," he says. "Today, I edit the shoots electronically using Photomechanic and Photoshop CS2 on Mac G5 computers, adjust exposures and color balances, and produce proofs for the client either online or on a DVD. This can take anywhere from a few hours to a day to produce. Clients then make their selections (and whenever I can I will try to help guide their selections). Then I do the digital processing and retouching/enhancing of the selected RAW files to produce the images for reproduction. This can be as simple as a five-minute procedure on some images or can involve an entire day's work on other images depending upon the desired look. Digital imaging has allowed for control never before possible, but it has increased the post-shoot workflow tremendously. Most days where I am not actually shooting I probably spend 40 to 70 percent of the time editing and retouching on the computer." Eric spends the balance of his day speaking with clients either in person or on the phone, answering e-mails, putting together proposals and bids, and handling other tasks. "When you add this all together it frequently makes for 60- to 70-hour work weeks (and sometimes more)," he says.

To Be a Successful Fashion Photographer, You Should . . .

- have excellent manual dexterity, good eyesight and color vision, and artistic ability
- be skilled at using digital cameras, computer software programs, and related technology
- have an eye for detail
- be able to work under deadline pressure
- have a strong interest in fashion
- be willing to work long hours to meet deadlines and to achieve your artistic goals
- have good business skills if you own your own business
- have confidence in your abilities and artistic vision

HAVE I GOT WHAT IT TAKES TO BE A FASHION PHOTOGRAPHER?

Photographers need excellent manual dexterity, good eyesight and color vision, and artistic ability (able to visualize designs, use colors, and create style). They need an eye for composition as well as the ability to work creatively with their chosen medium. Fashion photographers need to be adept at using technologies such as digital cameras and various computer programs designed to manipulate photographs. Because they work with groups of people, they will need to be patient, accommodating, and professional. An eye for detail is essential. They also need to be able to work under deadline pressure. "It can be exciting and very challenging trying to create something new and fresh while under tight deadlines," Eric says. And, naturally, fashion photographers should be interested in fashion and expressing style through images.

Aspiring fashion photographers need to keep in mind that amid the glamour of photographing well-known models or travel to exotic locales for a photo shoot is a career that requires a lot of hard work, dedication, and long hours. "Photography is a lot of work, long hours on the computer, not as glamorous as people might imagine, and the money can be very up and down," Eric says. "This is an extremely competitive business, and financial pressures can get in the way of creativity and inspiration if one is not careful."

HOW DO I BECOME A FASHION PHOTOGRAPHER?

Education

High School

Creativity is probably the most important skill for success in this field. There are a number of classes you can take in high school to help you determine the extent of your talent as well as prepare you for this work. Naturally, take as many photography classes as you can, as well as fashion-related classes if they are offered. Also, take computer classes that teach you how to use photo manipulation

> **Useful Web Site**
>
> **Fashion Net: How to Become a Fashion Photographer**
> http://www.fashion.net/howto/photography

software. Business, accounting, or mathematics classes will give you skills you will need to keep track of your accounts and run your own business. Take English or communication classes to develop your communication skills. You will be working with a variety of people, often as a member of a team, and you must be able to convey your ideas clearly as well as accurately follow directions.

Postsecondary Training

Although this is a career field in which you don't need to take a specific postsecondary educational route, there are a number of training options available. There are, for example, academic programs in fashion photography at many colleges, universities, and adult education centers. Some community and junior colleges offer associate degrees in photography or commercial art. Photography studies will include shooting and processing techniques using both black-and-white and color film, digital technology, lighting, and composition. An advantage to pursuing education beyond high school is that it gives you an opportunity to build your portfolio. A portfolio is a collection of an artist's best work that shows prospective clients a variety of skills.

In addition to studying art and photography, it is advantageous to study clothing construction, fabrics, fashion design, and cosmetology.

Internships and Volunteerships

If you attend a postsecondary program, you will be required to participate in an internship, which is typically unpaid and lasts anywhere from 4 to 12 months. As an intern, you might work as a photographer's assistant at a fashion magazine, a fashion house, or in another fashion-related setting. This experience will allow you to work closely with fashion photographers and other industry professionals and learn more about the pros and cons of the field.

If you are still in high school, you can volunteer to take photographs for your school newspaper or literary magazine. You can also look for part-time or summer work (or a volunteer opportunity) at a camera store. These experiences will give you the opportunity to become familiar with many "tools of the trade."

WHO WILL HIRE ME?

If you have received a degree, one of the best ways to start out in this business is to find a job through your school's career services office or by networking with alumni. Those who are interested in photography sometimes gain entry by working as assistants or trainees to established photographers. You may be asked to do such things as move lights, work in the darkroom, and schedule appointments, but you will also gain experience and make contacts in

What Makes for a Successful Fashion Photograph

The editors of *What Can I Do Now?: Fashion* asked Eric Stephenson to describe the components of a successful fashion photograph: "The most important elements of a successful fashion photograph are strong graphic composition and emotion. Effective use of lighting and color play into this. For a shoot to be effective, photographers need to have clear ideas of the look and emotions they are trying to bring forth. They then need to translate this vision to film (or digital) by their choice of how to light the photographs, types of backgrounds, and by the compositional styles they wish to employ. It helps to have good communication with the models so they also understand the desired looks. Of course the other critical element is to produce images that meet with the client's needs."

the field. Those who are financially able may go into business for themselves right away. However, it may take considerable time to establish yourself in the field and have a business that is profitable.

More than 50 percent of all professional photographers are self-employed. Others work for large retailers, magazines, newspapers, design or advertising firms, and fashion firms (called *houses*).

While Eric was taking formal photography courses at a local community college, he began assisting several commercial photographers, and eventually began to take on freelance assignments shooting furniture, architecture, editorial, and catalog work. "I eventually was hired as a staff photographer for the Denver Art Museum and photographed painting and sculpture for books and magazines," he says. "While at the museum I also worked on a number of personal and freelance assignments and attended evening classes at the University of Colorado-Denver to earn an MBA in preparation for starting my own photographic business. Running a successful photography business takes a mixture of artistic, technical, business, and people and networking skills, which are probably not encompassed by a single degree or course of study."

WHERE CAN I GO FROM HERE?

Advancement for fashion photographers generally comes as they gain professional recognition. Freelance photographers who become known for the creativity and high quality of their work will have a growing client base. More clients translate into more jobs; more jobs translate into higher earnings. In addition, as photographers become better known, they can charge more for their services and be more selective about what jobs they take. Salaried photographers may either move up within their organization, taking on supervisory roles or working with specific accounts for example, or they may choose to start their own photography business.

Where does Eric see himself in 5 or 10 years? "Ideally," he says, "I would like my business to grow enough to allow me to hire more help so I can focus more on just creating the images and less on running the business. I would also like to get to the point financially where I can be more selective in the assignments that I am undertaking. I would like to be working on less of the bread and butter assignments that pay the bills, but allow for little creativity."

Related Jobs

- art photographers
- cinematographers and directors of photography
- fashion coordinators
- fashion illustrators
- fashion photography instructors
- fashion stylists
- medical photographers
- photo editors
- photo stylists
- photographic equipment technicians
- photojournalists
- portrait photographers
- sports photographers
- wedding photographers

WHAT ARE THE SALARY RANGES?

According to the U.S. Department of Labor, the median annual earnings for salaried photographers was approximately $26,080 in 2004. The lowest paid 10 percent made less than $15,000, while the highest paid 10 percent made more than $54,180 per year. Photographers who worked for newspaper, book, and directory publishers had mean annual earnings of $36,760 in 2004, and those employed by department stores earned $45,300.

Photographers running their own businesses and working on a freelance basis are typically paid by the job. The pay for these jobs may be based on such factors as the photographer's reputation, the prestige of the client (for example, a fashion magazine with an international readership will pay more than a local newspaper doing a Sunday fashion spread), and the difficulty of the work. For some of this work, photographers may make $250 per job. They may also get credit lines and receive travel expenses. As they gain experience, build a strong portfolio of published work, and have prestigious clients, photographers can make $2,000 per job or more. Freelance photographers who have national or international reputations may make hundreds of thousands of dollars or more per year. Freelance workers, unlike salaried artists, however, do not have benefits such as health insurance and paid vacation or sick days.

WHAT IS THE JOB OUTLOOK?

According to the U.S. Department of Labor, employment for visual artists and photographers is expected to grow as fast as the average through 2014. For photographers specifically working in fashion, employment will likely be dependent on the prosperity of organizations involved with the fashion field, such as magazines, newspapers, advertising firms, and fashion houses. The outlook for these organizations currently looks strong. The popularity of American fashions around the world should create a demand for photographers who can effectively capture the latest styles. In addition, numerous outlets for fashion, such as e-zines and retail Web sites, will create a need for photographers.

Competition for jobs, however, will be keen since these positions are highly attractive to people with artistic ability. In addition, the *Occupational Outlook Handbook* notes that the growing popularity of digital cameras and computer art programs can allow consumers and businesses to produce and access photographic images on their own. Despite this improved technology, the specialized skills of the trained photographer should still find demand in the fashion world. Individuals who are creative and persistent in finding job leads and who are able to adapt to rapidly changing technologies will be the most successful.

Fashion Stylists

SUMMARY

Definition
Fashion stylists work with photographers and other professionals to create a particular image, using props, backgrounds, accessories, clothing, costumes, food, linens, and other set elements.

Alternative Job Titles
Photo stylists

Salary Range
$16,000 to $30,000 to $50,000+

Educational Requirements
Some postsecondary training

Certification or Licensing
None available

Employment Outlook
About as fast as the average

High School Subjects
Art
Business
Family and consumer science

Personal Interests
Design
Photography

Scouting a beach location for a swimsuit shoot. Tracking down vintage beach chairs and the right color towels. Booking models and photographers. Working with industry professionals to ensure the appropriate "look" of a shoot. These are just a few of the tasks in the average day of a fashion stylist, a career that is an increasingly vital part of the fashion and advertising industries.

WHAT DOES A FASHION STYLIST DO?

The fashion stylist is a creative collaborator, working with photographers, art directors, models, design houses, and clients to produce a visual image, usually for commercial purposes. It is both a technical and artistic occupation. The kind of work a fashion stylist performs depends upon, among other things, the nature of the photography; the needs of the photographer, studio, and art director; and the requests of the client. Because these factors vary from one situation to another, it is impossible to list all the aspects of a fashion stylist's job. In simple terms, what a stylist does is help to create a "look." The specifics of how it is done are far more complicated.

Prop gathering and set decoration are the most common assignments in photo styling, but stylists have many other responsibilities, each requiring different skills and experience. Fashion, wardrobe, and portrait shoots, for example, often require a number of professional stylists on hand to scout locations, prepare the set, acquire clothes and accessories, dress the models, and style hair and makeup. *On-figure stylists* fit clothes to a model, and *off-figure stylists* arrange clothes in attractive stacks or against an interesting background. *Soft-goods stylists* introduce appropriate fabric, linens, and clothing into a shoot. *Hair and makeup stylists* are almost invariably cosmetic specialists, and are usually present on any set that employs live models. *Casting stylists* locate modeling talent.

Stylists may also bring special talents to the set, like floral design, gift-wrapping, model-building, or antiquing. They usually have a "bag of tricks" that will solve problems or create certain effects; a stylist's work kit might include everything from duct tape and cotton wadding to C-clamps and saltshakers. Sometimes a photo stylist is called on to design and build props, perform on-set, last-minute tailoring, even coordinate the entire production from the location search to crew accommodations. The most successful stylists will adapt to the needs of the job, and if they can't produce something themselves, they will know in an instant how and where to find someone who can. Versatility and flexibility are key attributes, no matter what the stylist's specialty.

Being prepared for every possible situation is a large part of the fashion stylist's job. Knowledge of photographic techniques, especially lighting, lenses, and filters, can help a stylist communicate better with the photographer. An understanding of the advertising and fashion industries and familiarity with specific product lines and designers are also good tools for working with clients.

Organization is another vital aspect of the fashion stylist's job. Before the shoot, the stylist must be sure that everything needed has been found and will arrive on time at the studio or location. During the shoot, even while working on a model or set, the stylist must be sure that all borrowed materials are being treated with care and that preparations for the next shot are underway. Afterwards, he or she must return items and maintain receipts and records, so as to keep the project within budget. The freelance stylist does all this while also rounding up new assignments and maintaining a current portfolio.

Only part of the stylist's time is spent in photo studios or on location. Much of the work is done on the phone and on the street, preparing for the job by gathering props and materials, procuring clothes, contacting models, or renting other items. For the freelancer, lining up future employment can be a job in itself. A senior stylist working in-house at a magazine may have additional editorial duties, including working with art directors to introduce concepts and compose advertising narratives.

Even during downtime, the stylist must keep an eye out for ways to enhance his or her marketability. The chance discovery of a new boutique or specialty shop on the way to the grocery store can provide the stylist with a valuable new resource for later assignments. Maintaining a personal directory of resources is as essential as keeping a portfolio. Staying abreast of current trends and tastes through the media is also important, especially in the areas of fashion and lifestyle.

What a stylist does on the job depends largely upon his or her unique talents and abilities. Fashion stylists with the most experience and creative resources will make the greatest contribution to a project. As a premier stylist, that contribution extends beyond the set to society as a whole: shaping its tastes, making its images, and creating art that defines the era.

Photo Stylist Specialties

In addition to fashion styling, there are many other types of stylists working in the field, according to the Association of Stylists and Coordinators. The following list details the various specialties in what is generically known as photo styling. It is important to note that the duties of fashion stylists overlap with some of these fields.

- advertising
- bedding
- bridal
- casting and production
- catalog
- children
- costumes
- editorial
- film, video, and commercials
- food
- jewelry
- lifestyle (sometimes called illustration)
- set design and interiors
- softgoods
- special talents
- still life
- tabletop
- visual merchandising
- wardrobe

WHAT IS IT LIKE TO BE A FASHION STYLIST?

Susan Kroeter is a freelance fashion stylist in New York City. She has worked in the field for 18 years. Susan says that there is no typical day for a fashion stylist. "It really depends on what I'm doing and where and when, while I'm in the job process," she says. "After I'm hired for a job, I get the dates for the photo shoot and discuss the talent [models, photographers, etc.] the client wants to reserve tentatively for the job. I call all the talent agencies and hold the time on the talent. I work closely with the client to go over the layouts that pertain to the upcoming photo shoot. It's there we see what we are going to shoot and what the client is trying to sell in their catalog. There is also a lot of shopping and coordinating involved; for example, I have to get props and wardrobe for the photo shoot. I try to rent when I can, or I may have to buy what I need. We shoot lifestyle pictures sometimes and they require [realistic] looking sets, and the talent needs to be doing something to lend real life to the pictures. I buy or rent activity-type items that the customer can relate to, like drinking coffee, so I buy coffee cups. Sometimes we have the model paint, so someone has to get the supplies for the pictures, and that is my job, as well as getting clothing that we need to complete an outfit. In terms of coordinating, maybe the client isn't selling all the parts; for example, they are selling a line of blouses but they are not selling pants. I have to coordinate the outfits with wardrobe so we can sell the product.

"Once all of these issues have been addressed, the shots get assigned to each model and we make a plan about which merchandise will get shot together and where. We then arrange to go on location to shoot the shots we've been hired to produce."

Work conditions for a fashion stylist are as varied as the job itself. Preparation for a shoot may involve hours on the telephone, calling from the home or office, and more hours shopping for props and materials to use on the set. Much of the work is done inside comfortable photo studios or at other indoor locations, but sometimes, especially in fashion and catalog photography, outdoor locations are also used. If the merchandise is of a seasonal nature, this could mean long days working in a cold field photographing winter parkas against a snowy background, or it could mean flying down to Key West in January for a week shooting next summer's line of swimwear. Travel, both local and long distance, is part of the job. Susan says that she travels quite a bit for her job, "and we always go somewhere sunny with good weather." Days can be long, from dawn to dusk, or they may require the stylist's presence for only a few hours on the set. Hours vary, but a stylist must always be flexible, especially the freelancer who may be called in on a day's notice.

Stress levels vary from one assignment to the next. Some shoots may go smoothly, others may have a crisis occur every minute. Stylists must be able to remain calm and resilient in the face of enormous pressure. Personality clashes may also occur despite every effort to avoid them, adding to the stress of the job. For the freelancer, the pressures to find new work and maintain proper business records are still further sources of stress. Fashion stylists will also spend considerable time on their feet, stooping and kneeling in uncomfortable positions or trying to get something aligned just right. They also may need to transport heavy material and merchandise to and from the studio or location or move these elements around the set during the shoot. Reliable transportation is essential.

The irregular hours of a fashion stylist can be an attraction for people who enjoy variety in their lives. Work conditions are not always that strenuous. The work can also be pleasant and fun, as the crew trades jokes and experiences, solves problems together, and shares the excitement of a sudden inspiration. The rewards of working with a team of professionals on an interesting, creative project is a condition of the job that most stylists treasure.

DO I HAVE WHAT IT TAKES TO BE A FASHION STYLIST?

Susan believes that the most important skills for a fashion stylist are "kindness to others (there is a lot of people contact in this field), patience (sometimes things go wrong or take longer than planned), the ability to be punctual (that usually goes with being professional), and standing up for yourself (some people thinks it's okay to renegotiate a contract during a shoot that isn't going well). Having good taste, a good eye, and the ability to shop like you're participating in a scavenger hunt against the clock are also good qualities."

In addition, schedules in this career can be hectic and work is not always done during normal business hours, so stylists need flexibility and the ability to work under pressure. Stylists who are easy to work with often find that they have a large number of clients. Finally, an eye for detail is a must. Stylists are responsible for making sure that everything appearing in a photo—from a model's hairstyle to the size and color of a lamp—is exactly right.

To Be a Successful Fashion Stylist, You Should . . .

- be able to work well with others
- have patience and creativity in the event that shoots do not go as planned
- have strong negotiation skills
- have excellent taste and an eye for style and the latest fashion trends
- be able to work well under pressure
- have confidence in your professional abilities
- have strong business acumen

HOW DO I BECOME A FASHION STYLIST?

Education

High School

There are a number of classes you can take to help prepare for this career while you are still in high school. Take classes in the visual arts to learn about design and composition. Develop your hand-eye coordination in sculpture or pottery classes where you will be producing three-dimensional objects. Painting classes will teach you about colors, and photography classes will give you a familiarity using this medium. Skill with fabric is a must, so take family and consumer science classes that concentrate on fabric work. You will be able to cultivate your skills pressing and steaming clothes, doing minor alterations, and completing needlework. Because your work as a fashion stylist may require you to work as a freelancer (running your own business), take mathematics classes or business and accounting classes that will prepare you to keep your own financial records. Of course, English classes are important. English classes will give you the communication skills that you will need to work well with a variety of people, to promote your own work, and to drum up new business. The specialties employed for certain shoots require a familiarity with, for instance, formal attire, food preparation, home decorating, children, bedding, and any number of other potential subjects. A fashion stylist, like any artist, draws from his or her own experience for inspiration, so exposure to a wide variety of experiences will benefit anyone entering the field.

Postsecondary Training

There is no specific postsecondary educational or training route you must take to enter this field. Some fashion schools, such as the Fashion Institute of Technology, offer training in fabric styling. Other fashion stylists have attended art schools, receiving degrees in photography; attended fashion schools, receiving degrees in fashion merchandising or a related field; or have entered the field by going into retail, working for large department stores, for example, to gain experience with advertising, marketing, and even product display. The Association of Stylists and Coordinators (ASC) recommends entering the field by working as an assistant for an established stylist. Susan agrees with this recommendation. "Studying photography in college has been helpful," she says, "but I assisted a stylist and got on-the-job training, which is the best training for a career as a stylist." According to the ASC, such an informal apprenticeship usually lasts about two years. By then, the assistant typically has enough skills and connections to begin working on his or her own.

Internships and Volunteerships

If you attend college, you will most likely be required to participate in an internship in the fashion industry—perhaps even with a fashion stylist. Internships, which usually last from 4 to 12 months, are typically unpaid, but count toward college credit.

If you're still in high school, look for part-time or summer work in the retail field, where you may have the opportunity to set up displays and learn about advertising. Even if you can't find such work, watch someone prepare a display in a department store window. Many stylists start out as window dressers or doing in-store display work.

WHO WILL HIRE ME?

Susan says that she fell into the career of fashion stylist by accident. "I went to school for photography and moved to New York to work as an assistant to a photographer," she explains. "I had done a little styling (getting props) when I lived in Philadelphia, but I didn't know that this was what I was doing. When I got to New York, the photographer I was supposed to work for was in Milan, and he told me to 'temp' until he returned. We eventually met for brunch, and he told me that he was staying in Milan indefinitely, hence no job. While I was temping, I saw an ad in the *New York Times* for an assistant to a stylist and photographer. Out of 85 people who applied, I got the job."

A person can enter the field of photo styling at any point in life, but there is no clear-cut way to go about it. Some people, if they have the resources, hire photographers to shoot a portfolio with them, then shop it around to production houses and other photographers. Most prospective employers, however, prefer that a stylist has previous on-set experience.

As the ASC recommends, one of the best ways to break into this field is to find work as a stylist's assistant. Production houses and photo studios that employ full-time stylists usually keep a directory of assistants. Most cities have a creative directory of established stylists who may need assistants. It is important to always leave a name and number; they may have no work available immediately, but might be desperate for help next month. Working as an assistant will provide you with important on-set experience as well as show you the nuts and bolts of the job—including the drudgery along with the rewards. Building a reputation is the most important thing to do at any stage of this career, since most photographers find stylists by word of mouth and recommendations, as well as by reviewing portfolios. Assistants will also be introduced to the people who may hire them down the road as full-fledged stylists, giving them an opportunity to make a good impression. Eventually, you can seek out a photographer who needs a stylist and work together on test shots. Once you have enough examples of your work for a portfolio, you can show it to agents, editors, and photographers.

Agency representation can be of enormous help to the freelancer. An agent finds work for the stylist and pays him or her on a regular basis (after extracting an average commission of 20 percent). The benefit of representation is that while a stylist is working one job, the agent is lining up the next. Some agencies represent stylists exclusively; others also handle models, photographers, and actors.

There are relatively few positions available for full-time, salaried fashion stylists. Some ad agencies, magazines, and companies that sell their merchandise through catalogs have stylists on staff. Most fashion stylists, however, work as freelancers. Photographers, ad agencies, design firms, catalog houses, and any other enterprise that uses photographic services hire them for individual assignments.

WHERE CAN I GO FROM HERE?

Advancement in this field can be measured by the amount of bookings a stylist obtains, the steadiness of work, and a regularly increasing pay rate. It can also be determined by the quality of a stylist's clients, the reputation of the photographer, and the nature of the assignments. Some stylists start out with lower-end catalogs and work their way up. If the goal is to do high fashion, then the steps along the way will be readily apparent in the quality of the merchandise and the size of the client. The opportunity to work with highly regarded photographers is also a step up, even if the stylist's pay rate remains the same. In a career built on reputation, experience with the industry's major players is priceless. Senior stylists at magazines often help in ad design and planning. Some stylists advance to become art directors and fashion editors. Ultimately, each stylist

Related Jobs

- art directors
- cosmetologists
- fashion coordinators
- fashion editors and writers
- fashion illustrators
- fashion photographers
- merchandise displayers
- photo editors

has his or her own goals in sight. The "rare-air" of high fashion and celebrity photography may not be the end-all for all stylists; a good steady income and the chance to work regularly with friendly, creative people may, in fact, be of more importance to a stylist.

WHAT ARE THE SALARY RANGES?

Like almost everything else in this field, earning potential varies from one stylist to the next. Salaries at production houses can start as low as $8 an hour, but usually include fringe benefits like health insurance, not to mention a regular paycheck. The freelancer, on the other hand, has enormous earning potential. An experienced fashion stylist can demand as much as $800 or more a day, depending on his or her reputation and the budget of the production. Regular bookings at this level translate into a substantial income.

Most stylists, however, earn less and average approximately $350 to $500 per day. According to the ASC, assistant stylists, who are hired by the day, can expect to make approximately $150 to $200 per day. Neither assistants nor stylists who are freelancers receive any kind of benefits. They must provide for their own health insurance and retirement, and they receive no pay for sick days or vacation days. In addition, while a stylist may have a job that pays $500 a day for several days, there is no assurance that a stylist will find steady employment. It is wise to establish an emergency fund in the event that work disappears for a time. Busy periods often correspond to seasonal advertising campaigns and film work. A stylist might have a great year followed by a disappointing one. Freelancers must file their own quarterly tax returns and purchase their own health insurance.

WHAT IS THE JOB OUTLOOK?

The value of a good fashion stylist is becoming more and more apparent to photographers and advertising clients. The outlook for employment for stylists, however, depends a great deal on their perseverance and reputation. Larger cities are the most fertile places to find work, but there are photo studios in nearly every community. The fortunes of the stylist are intrinsically related to the health of the fashion, advertising, film, video, and commercial photography industries—all of which are in good shape. Stylists should try, however, to maintain a wide client base if possible, so they can be assured of regular work in case one source dries up.

Technological advances, especially in the areas of digital photography and photo enhancement, may transform, but not eliminate, the role of the photo stylist in the future. Someday there may be educational avenues for the stylist to enter into the field, and this may increase the amount of competition for styling assignments. Ultimately, though, maintaining the quality of work is the best insurance for continued employment.

Makeup Artists

SUMMARY

Definition
Makeup artists prepare models and actors for performances on stage and before cameras.

Alternative Job Titles
None

Salary Range
$13,410 to $24,410 to $63,640+

Educational Requirements
Some postsecondary training

Certification or Licensing
None available

Employment Outlook
Faster than the average

High School Subjects
Art
Business
Chemistry
Theater

Personal Interests
Design
Helping people: personal service
Photography
Theater

Sometimes it's what you *don't* do that gets you noticed: just ask makeup artist Rachael Perrin. Recently, she was the key artist for a major fashion show in Chicago, Illinois. "I was asked to care for the emcee for the evening," she recalls, "who just happened to be a supermodel and actress. I realized she needed to memorize some of the information for the show, and that she was using her time in my chair as the calm before the storm. So I gave her that time and kept the conversation to a minimum, which is exactly what she needed at that moment."

"After I did her makeup, she joined her publicist and agent to go over details for the following day. They were all pleased with my work and decided to hire me to do her makeup the next morning for her TV appearances, which is a major resume booster.

"The moral of the story is to treat all of your clients with respect and kindness. Like in sales, every person you meet is a potential client or referral. This business is all about reputation and yours is only as good as your last few jobs."

WHAT DOES A MAKEUP ARTIST DO?

Makeup artists who work in the fashion industry prepare models for photo shoots, fashion shows, and other fashion industry events. They often collaborate with designers to create makeup and hair "looks" for seasonal collections. In addition to applying makeup, in smaller markets, makeup artists are often responsible for styling hair, extensions, and wigs. Outside of the fashion industry, makeup artists are employed in the motion picture, television, and commercial industries, as well as in theatrical productions.

Long hours, deadlines, and tight budgets can create high stress in nearly any production in which a makeup artist is involved. Because makeup artists move from fashion shoot to theatre production to movie set, they work with different groups of people all the time, and in different locales and settings. Although this allows makeup artists the opportunity to travel, it may also make a makeup artist feel displaced. While working on a production, they may have to forgo a social life, working long hours to design effects and prepare the models and actors. Production workdays can be twice as long as in the average workplace, and those work hours may be a stressful combination of working hurriedly then waiting. For those passionate about the work, however, any uncomfortable or frustrating conditions are easily overlooked.

WHAT IS IT LIKE TO BE A MAKEUP ARTIST?

Rachael Perrin has been a professional makeup artist for three and a half years. "I was in love with makeup as a child," she says, "and absolutely loved all of my art classes in school. Applying makeup on other people came very naturally to me, and in high school I was the one who set the makeup trend among my peers. For example, when everyone else was stuck in the 'blue frosty shadow phase' back in the mid '80s, I had already moved on to mint green and black-rimmed eyes. I believe it was just meant to be. I hear similar stories from almost every successful artist that I work with, so it just goes to show that childhood dreams can turn into reality. But I realize that it's a career, just like any other. It takes a lot of hard work and dedication, but I wouldn't trade the worst day in the makeup field for the best day in corporate America."

Rachael says that she has no typical days since she works in such a variety of settings. "For example, my day on a commercial set usually begins with a 7:00 or 8:00 A.M. call-time. Depending on the needs of the client, I might be busy all day or I might spend a lot of time sitting around waiting to do touchups," she says. "It's important to bring a few magazines or a book to keep yourself busy. Luckily, I am completely wireless so that I can check e-mail and view the Web wherever I am. In this field, jobs come and go in the blink of an eye, so it's imperative to be accessible to your clients. On a fashion shoot, I may be busy the entire day with little time for a break. Working a runway show is a three- to five-hour commitment the day of the shoot, but includes more preparation time if you are the key artist. And a day at a department store is nonstop, on your feet selling for up to eight hours. There are so many variations to my week, but I prefer to do makeup in a variety of settings."

To Be a Successful Makeup Artist, You Should . . .

- have patience and the ability to work well with others
- be attentive to detail
- have an artistic sensibility
- be able to work well under deadline pressure
- have business acumen
- be able to accept constructive criticism regarding your work
- be persistent and confident of your abilities

In addition to her artistic responsibilities, Rachael handles all of her own administrative tasks such as updating her portfolio and Web sites, shopping for supplies in stores and online, managing her calendar, running errands, and invoicing clients. "You are truly your own assistant when it comes to paperwork," she says. "So you must use your time wisely, especially when busy. It's easy to forget to send an invoice to a client, and it's also easy for them to forget to pay you."

Some makeup artists travel for their work, but Rachael says that it's not always necessary if you live in a big city. "I have some clients that prefer that I travel to them," she says. "Others come to Chicago to work with me, but most are local. However, when an artist hits a certain level of success, more and more travel may be necessary—and who wouldn't enjoy a week in Paris for the major shows, then a couple of weeks in Miami in the dead of winter? "

Rachael truly loves her job. "There are so many aspects of my job that are absolutely amazing. I get to make my own schedule, to some extent. And generally I get to choose which jobs I want to work, and which I don't. I get to be backstage at runway shows and see my name in print. And I get to collaborate with art directors, producers, photographers, fashion designers, and models on some pretty amazing projects. And now that my work is getting published, cosmetic lines have started sending me makeup to use in my print work, and others send skin and hair care products for me to try out and review. Not to mention the industry discounts available for all makeup artists from MAC, NARS, Smashbox, and a multitude of other lines."

DO I HAVE WHAT IT TAKES TO BE A MAKEUP ARTIST?

Patience and the ability to get along well with people are important for a makeup artist—throughout a production, the actors will spend many hours in the makeup chair. Though many models and actors will be easy to work with, you may have to put up with much irritability, as well as overwhelming egos. Fashion coordinators, photographers, producers, and directors can also be difficult to work with. And, as you gain more experience, you may have more knowledge about your particular field than those who are

Tips for Success from Makeup Artist Rachael Perrin

- If you have a strong aptitude for art, enjoy working with a variety of people in a variety of environments, and don't mind doing a lot of grunt work to build your portfolio, then makeup artistry might just be the career for you. Remember, though, that makeup artistry is a career. If you want to work as a freelance artist, you will be in charge of your own schedule, accounting, and more. And unless you work full time at a makeup counter or in a salon, you may have difficulty getting benefits. Paychecks usually come in slowly. If you work only on a freelance basis, bookings can be a 'feast or famine' situation. You could be beyond busy for weeks, and then suddenly have a week that's simply empty.
- Due to the phenomenon of the glamorous 'celebrity makeup artist,' many people are entering this field with stars in their eyes. But there are no shortcuts to success. For every well-known makeup artist, there are hundreds of nameless makeup artists working at makeup counters and salons, as well as doing freelance work in smaller markets. Unless you plan to move to New York or Los Angeles, or have unlimited funds to invest in a cosmetic line, your chances of becoming the next Bobbi Brown are very small.
- Startup costs can also be quite expensive. It's not uncommon to spend several thousand dollars while building your makeup kit. Look for good deals on brushes and tools and buy your supplies in bulk whenever possible. Makeup artists get discounts on several lines once they have proof that they are actively working in the field. Look for discounts and sales. Instead of buying all prestige brands, search makeup artist forums for quality lines that are less expensive. If you ask politely, most artists will share some industry secrets with you.
- Focus on the basics when you are getting started. Until you can effortlessly match foundation to all skin tones, pick color for all skin shades, and perfectly highlight and contour different eye and face shapes, you will have a difficult time completing the most basic of jobs. Many new artists make the mistake of focusing on avant-garde makeup, and try to bypass the creation of clean images. Skip the theatrical, edgy, and creative makeup and work on creating a clean beauty portfolio that will impress agencies, photographers, and potential clients.

in charge of the event. This may put you in frustrating situations, and you may see time wasted in costly mistakes. Rachael says that it's important to remember that each person is hired to do a particular job: "If you are hired to do makeup, you are not the director or producer. If you step on other people's toes, then you will be remembered as the difficult one. It's important to look at every gig as a chance to learn and grow."

Attention to detail is important; you must be quick to spot any makeup problems before a model hits the runway or begins filming. Such responsibilities can be stressful—a whole fashion production team will be relying on you to properly apply makeup that will look good on the runway or on film. If your work isn't up to par, the whole production will suffer. Makeup artist work requires as much creativity and ingenuity as any task. Because of the tough, competitive nature of the fashion and entertainment industries, makeup artists must be persistent and enthusiastic in their pursuit of projects.

As a makeup artist, you may want to consider joining a union. The International Alliance of Theatrical Stage Employees (IATSE) represents workers in theater, film, and television production. Hair stylists, makeup artists, engineers, art directors, and set designers are some of the professionals who belong to the 500 local unions affiliated with IATSE. Union membership is not required of most makeup artists for film and theater, but it can help individuals negotiate better wages, benefits, and working conditions. Theaters in larger cities may require union membership of makeup artists, while smaller, regional theaters across the country are less likely to require membership.

HOW DO I BECOME A MAKEUP ARTIST?

Education

High School

There are a number of classes you can take in high school to help prepare for this profession. Take all the art classes you can, including art history if this is offered at your school. Photography courses will help you understand the use of light and shadow. Courses in illustration, painting, and drawing will help you to develop the skills you'll need for illustrating proposed makeup effects. Other helpful classes are anatomy and chemistry. Anatomy will give you an understanding of the human body, and chemistry will give you insight into the products you will be using. If your school offers drama classes, be sure to take these. Computer classes provide exposure to technology and various software, which you may use in the future to create designs. Finally, because this work is typically done on a freelance basis and you will need to manage your business accounts, it will be helpful for you to take math, business, and accounting classes.

You should also try experimenting with makeup on your own. Have professional photographs taken of your efforts to help you begin building a portfolio of your work. "Young people need to keep in mind that a portfolio of work needs to be shot professionally," Rachael advises. "Industry professionals won't look at images that you shoot yourself, or images of makeup you have done on your own face."

Postsecondary Training

There are a number of postsecondary educational routes you can take to become a makeup artist. If you have experience and a portfolio to show off your work, you may be able to enter the business right out of high school. This route is not always advisable, however, because your

Makeup Challenges

Makeup artists work in a variety of settings—from fashion shows and shoots to film, television, and theater productions. The editors of *What Can I Do Now?: Fashion* asked makeup artist Rachael Perrin to detail the challenges and tasks that are involved in each type of work.

Runway/Backstage: When working backstage at fashion/runway shows, you may not have the best lighting, the models might be running late, and if there are several designers taking part in the show, they may all want different makeup and hair 'looks.' So it's important to understand the flow of the show, which designer is on first, and how to handle quick changes backstage in between each run. A mistake that I see a lot of new makeup artists make at shows is to do their work, and then run out to watch the show. Unfortunately, seeing the show is not always a possibility. Most likely, you will be working with a key artist, who determines who needs to remain backstage, and often they will want to remain backstage to ensure that the models look perfect. In that case, they may want the newer artists out front to view the show and give feedback. In short, never assume anything!

Photography/Print: When you are scheduled to do a photo shoot, make sure to get all of the details. Know what style of makeup you will be doing and what products and tools you will need. You won't get a second chance if you are late, cancel last minute, or show up unprepared to do your work. It's also important to remember that each photographer works differently. Some will want you involved in each shot, making sure every hair is in place, while others will want you to stay off set once you have finished your work. If you want to get booked for a second shoot, it's important to communicate with the photographer and to accommodate his or her work style.

TV/Film Production: When working in a production environment, it's very important to learn your reporting structure. There are so many people on set, from producer to director to talent. Knowing who's who on set can really make your day run smoothly. You also need to understand the effects of color on your work. When working in a 'blue screen' environment, it's imperative that you keep the colors warm or the talent will look they crawled out of the grave. A green screen has a similar effect. The more you know about your settings, the more successful you will be in getting booked for future productions.

chances for establishing a successful freelance career without further training are slim. You must be very ambitious, enthusiastic, and capable of seeking out successful mentors willing to teach you the ropes. This can mean a lot of time working for free or for very little pay.

Another route you can take is to get specific training for makeup artistry through vocational schools. One advantage of this route is that after graduating from the program, you will be able to use the school's career services office, instructors, and other graduates as possible networking sources for jobs. In addition to completing her bachelor's degree, Rachael attended a five-month, hands-on training program at Columbia College in Chicago. "It included makeup for print, runway, theater, and bridal," she says. "I was also trained in corrective makeup."

A third route you can take is to get a broad-based college or university education that results in either a bachelor's or master's degree. Popular majors for makeup artists include theater, art history, film history, photography, and fashion merchandising. In addition to makeup courses, it is important to take classes in painting, illustration, computer design, and animation. A master of fine arts degree in theater or filmmaking will allow you to gain hands-on experience in production as well as working with a faculty of practicing artists.

In addition to formal education, makeup artists need to continue to learn about new styles, techniques, and products throughout their careers. "Since my initial training program, I have taken a few seminars from MAC Cosmetics," Rachael says. "I have also been trained on a variety of luxury and brand-name, retail-cosmetic lines. I also freelance for a number of cosmetic lines, so that I get advance notice of the latest products before they hit the shelves. Not to mention that I get the opportunity to use the products the minute they hit the store shelves, and can then advise my personal clientele on what's hot for the season." Rachael also studies the high-fashion magazines and the runway shows to stay ahead of the trends. "There are many sites that publish images from the ready-to-wear and couture shows, and the spring looks are usually available online in September," she says. "Generally the makeup and hair trends are showcased along with the designer's lines."

Internships and Volunteerships

Most postsecondary training programs provide internships, which give students the opportunity to gain firsthand experience at fashion studios, film and television production companies, and other venues.

High school drama departments or local community theaters can provide you with great opportunities to explore the makeup artist's work. Volunteer to assist with makeup during a stage production and you will learn about the materials and tools of a makeup kit, as well as see your work under stage lights. A high school video production team or film department may also offer you opportunities for makeup experience. Rachael suggests that those who are interested in doing makeup in the fashion industry should offer to assist a makeup artist working in print or runway. "If you only get the opportunity to clean their brushes," she says, "you will still learn more in one day than you could learn reading a dozen how-to makeup books."

WHO WILL HIRE ME?

Although makeup artists work in a wide variety of circumstances, from fashion and theater to television and movies, they usually are self-employed, contracting individual jobs. Theater troupes, touring shows, and amusement parks may hire makeup artists onto their staffs, but in the fashion, film, and television industries, makeup artists usually work on a freelance basis. Large cities and metropolitan areas will provide the majority of jobs for makeup artists, particularly those cities associated with the fashion industry, modeling/talent agencies, thriving theaters, or movie or television studios. Although there may be some jobs in smaller towns, they will be mostly along the lines of industrial films, corporate videos, and photographic shoots—not very promising for those who wish to make a living in this line of work. Those who aspire to work exclusively as makeup artists gravitate toward the big cities.

You should keep a photographic record of all the work you do for fashion, theater, and film productions, including photos of any drawings you've done for art classes. It's important to have a portfolio to send along with your resume to makeup departments, fashion coordinators, and producers. To build up a portfolio of photographs, offer to do makeup for local photographers on a "trade for print" basis. Check with local TV studios about work in their makeup departments. Locally produced newscasts, children's programming, documentaries, and commercials offer opportunities for makeup artists. Commercials are often quick productions (between one and three days) with small casts, and they pay well. Department stores hire makeup artists to demonstrate and sell cosmetic products in department stores, which may be a starting position for those who want to earn a salary while getting on-the-job training and practice.

Because of the freelance nature of the business, you'll be going from project to project. This requires you to constantly seek out work. Read industry trade magazines, and don't be shy about submitting your portfolio to fashion coordinators, producers, and studios. Self-promotion will be an important part of your success as a makeup artist.

WHERE CAN I GO FROM HERE?

Many makeup artists start as assistants or volunteers on a production, making contacts and connections. They eventually take on projects for which they are in charge of makeup departments and designing makeup effects.

Successful, experienced makeup artists can pick and choose their projects and work as much as they like. In the early years, makeup artists must frequently take on a variety of different projects just for the money; however, as they become established in the field and develop a solid reputation, they can concentrate on projects specific to their interests.

"Five years from now," Rachael predicts, "look for my name in the fashion and beauty magazines. They frequently quote artists with celebrity clientele on 'who's wearing what' and insider tips for application. And in 10 years, look for my name on the hottest fashion editorials in your favorite beauty and fashion magazines. That's where I see myself—working with the world's most talented photographers and beautiful models in the most exotic locales. You must have goals in this industry, or you will easily become stagnant, working with the same people over and over. In this industry, if you dream it and work towards it, you can be it."

Related Jobs

- barbers
- color analysts and image consultants
- cosmetics sales representatives
- cosmeticians
- cosmetologists
- fashion stylists
- mortuary cosmetologists
- nail technicians
- spa attendants
- special effects technicians

WHAT ARE THE SALARY RANGES?

Makeup artists usually contract with a production, negotiating a daily rate. This rate can vary greatly from project to project, depending on the budget of the production, the prestige of the project, and other factors. Even well-established makeup artists occasionally forgo payment to work on the low-budget independent productions of fashion designers or filmmakers they respect.

Independent contractors don't draw steady, yearly salaries. This means they may work long hours for several weeks, then, upon completion of a production, go without work for several weeks. Unless makeup artists are part of the union, they may be without benefits, having to provide their own health insurance. An experienced makeup artist can make around $500 a day on a film with a sizable budget, with assistants making around $200; some of the top makeup artists in the business command several thousand dollars each day. Theatrical makeup artists can make comparable daily wages on Broadway, or in a theater in a large city; some small theaters, however, may only pay around $50 a day. "In the fashion industry," Rachael says, "a makeup artist's day rate can range from $150 to $800 a day. When working with new designers, they may only be able to afford a $50 kit fee and trade for their designs. It's important to get everything in writing and to have someone knowledgeable look over your contract before you sign."

Because of such variables as the unsteady nature of the work, the makeup artist's experience, and even where he or she works, the yearly incomes for these individuals vary widely. Some makeup artists may show yearly earnings little higher than those resulting from the minimum wage. Others may have annual income in the hundreds of thousands of dollars. The U.S. Department of Labor reports that makeup artists (theatrical and performance) had median annual salaries of

$24,410 in 2004. Salaries ranged from less than $13,410 to more than $63,640; however, celebrity artists can earn salaries of more than $100,000 annually.

WHAT IS THE JOB OUTLOOK?

Makeup artists will find their opportunities increasing in the fashion, film, and television industries. The fashion industry continues to grow in popularity, and there will be a continuing need for makeup artists in still photography to prepare models for catalog and magazine shoots. Digital TV has made it possible for hundreds of cable channels to be piped into our homes. The original programming needed to fill the schedules of these new channels results in jobs for makeup artists. Makeup effects artists will find challenging and well-paying work as the film industry pushes the envelope on special effects. These makeup artists may be using computers more and more, as digital design becomes an important tool in creating film effects.

Funding for theaters, some of which comes from the National Endowment for the Arts, is always limited and may be reduced during economic downturns or when productions are unpopular. During these times many theaters may be unable to hire the cast and crew needed for new productions. There has been a revived interest in Broadway, however, due to highly successful musicals like *Rent* and *The Lion King*. This interest could result in better business for traveling productions, as well as regional theaters across the country.

Models

SUMMARY

Definition
Models display a wide variety of products and services in print, such as magazines and newspapers; television; and live marketing.

Alternative Job Titles
Artists' models
Fashion models
Floor models
Industrial models
Photographic models
Print models
Product demonstrators
Product promoters
Specialty models

Salary Range
$13,790 to $20,980 to $1 million+

Educational Requirements
High school diploma

Certification or Licensing
None available

Employment Outlook
About as fast as the average

High School Subjects
Business
Family and consumer science
Physical education
Speech
Theater

Personal Interests
Entertaining/performing
Exercise/personal fitness
Film and television
Photography
Travel

Although Josh Rigor, a print model in Chicago, Illinois, has worked on 16 shoots (including work for McDonald's, Sears, furniture companies, and public relations firms), he says that he still feels like the business is brand new to him. "Every experience is like walking into a college class and introducing yourself for the first time," he says. "I do feel more and more comfortable every time. I feel like I'm getting better at it. I always say to myself, 'I can't believe they are paying me!' I never sought out a career in modeling."

WHAT DOES A MODEL DO?

Models generally are grouped according to the medium or media in which they work; for instance, models who perform with movement in fashion shows and for retail stores (on the floor) are known as *fashion models.* Those who pose for artists are known as *artists' models,* and those who advertise products and services in print are known as *photographic models* or *print models.* In large cities there are modeling agencies that specialize in handling petite, plus-size, specialty, character, beauty, photographic, and high-fashion models.

Artists' models pose for individual artists or for classes of art students. When posing, models must stand or sit in one position for several hours at a time. A quick break for relaxation is usually given once each hour. Often the model must pose on a platform under hot and bright lights and sometimes wear little or no clothing. One job may last a day, while another may last for several weeks.

Photographic models pose for photographs. Their job is to lend attractiveness to an advertisement and enhance the desirability of the product. These models encounter a great variety of situations in their work. One series of photographs may be taken in a studio under hot lights with the model wearing a heavy fur coat. Another may be taken outdoors in midwinter with the model wearing only a bathing suit. One job may last only an hour, while another may require an entire day. In their work, models may travel to other states or even to other countries to be photographed in beautiful, unusual, or exotic settings.

Rarely do photographic models work full time. Days or weeks may pass between one job and the next, especially if they work on a freelance basis. If models contract with a modeling agency, however, their schedule may be fuller because the agency will be able to secure more modeling jobs for them.

The photographic model who has some acting ability may secure a job in a television commercial. These ads are usually videotaped or filmed. Although television modeling is very lucrative, it is very difficult for the average model to break into this field, mainly due to lack of training in acting.

Specialty models must possess particular features that are photogenic, such as hands, feet, legs, hair, lips, or ears that will help sell specific products.

Fashion models differ from the other types of models in three basic ways. First, the models usually work for clothing manufacturers, fashion designers, or department stores on a full-time basis. Second, they do not merely pose in one position, but walk around and assume a variety of poses in their display of the clothing. Third, they often speak to prospective purchasers to inform them of the model number and price of each garment.

Some fashion models may be employed by clothing manufacturers as showroom and fitting models. In many large department stores, a staff of full-time models is employed to promote the sale of various garments or accessories. The store may have a regularly scheduled style show during the daily lunch hour; at other times, models may walk throughout the store showing apparel and talking with customers about the garments and accessories being worn. Those models hired by a distributor to hand out free product samples, such as perfume or food, are known as *sampling demonstration models* or *product promoters.*

All fashion models employ certain techniques to display their clothing in the most effective way. Immaculate grooming is basic for most models, from the proper application of makeup and hair care to the smallest personal details. Models must walk gracefully with an erect carriage and master the techniques of pivoting to show the sides and back of a garment. They must know how to carry their hands and arms gracefully, as well as the body positions needed to emphasize certain details of their costume. They also must be able to call attention to accessories, such as purses, jewelry, and gloves.

Some fashion models do not work regularly but are called only for special style shows or certain buyers' showings. Some prefer to freelance since they may have other jobs or responsibilities. The most successful models work in all areas of the field, from live fashion modeling to print work to video and film modeling, as well as acting and live industrial and promotional presentations.

A Short History of Fashion Modeling

The story of fashion models begins in Paris, where they were first employed more than a century ago to display the exclusive clothing designed by French dressmakers for wealthy women. Before 1900, U.S. fashions were, for the most part, copies of the French originals, and it was seldom considered necessary for copied clothing to be shown by live models. Shortly after World War I, the U.S. garment industry created some original designs. These garments were mass-produced. As these fashion houses slowly multiplied, so did the number of models needed to show new clothing designs to prospective buyers. In the past 40 years, the U.S. garment industry has assumed world leadership in the production of clothing, and increasing numbers of models have been needed to display these garments and the fashion accessories that go with them.

WHAT IS IT LIKE TO BE A MODEL?

"I have been modeling consistently for one year," says Josh Rigor." "I say consistently because I did a modeling job about eight years ago. A friend of a friend's girlfriend was working as a photographer's assistant and said we, my friend and I, should go to an audition for Gingiss formalwear. Both my friend and I got the part playing high school seniors in a tuxedo advertisement. I didn't do another modeling job until last year."

Print models land jobs in the field in one of two ways: by attending casting calls (often known as "cattle calls" in the industry) or by establishing a reputation that allows them to forgo these casting calls and get hired directly by an employer. "I have a couple of agents," Josh says, "and I have never met a print model who doesn't have a minimum of three. My agent is contacted by a client who says, 'I want a 30-ish, urbanish yuppie.' And my agent will call me and give me the location and time of the audition. I go to the audition and fill out a form, which will have sections for name, agent, clothing measurements, phone number, and availability. The waiting room usually is filled with people waiting for their turn to take their test photo, which takes a

To Be a Successful Model, You Should . . .

- be able to work well with others
- have a freshness of face or manner
- have good health and physical stamina
- be tenacious when it comes to seeking employment opportunities
- be willing to work diligently to maintain your figure and appearance
- be able to accept constructive criticism regarding your "look" or modeling abilities

minute or two. After my test photo, I'm done. The longest part is waiting for your name to be called. A 30-ish, urban-ish yuppie can be anything: Caucasian, Black, Asian, Hispanic, 6-feet 5-inches tall, 5-feet 7-inches tall, long hair, buzz-cuts, Caesar's style with frosted tips, etc. Because the description of a possible model is so vague, an audition can take all day and involve hundreds of models. I hate cattle calls, and I usually don't go to them. A year ago I went to them all the time, but now I think that they are a waste of time.

"There are other ways to land jobs. If a client really likes me, then my agent will call me up and say that 'so and so wants you at this time. Are you available?' So in this case there is no competition with other models."

Josh rarely gets more than a day or two of notice that he will be needed for a shoot. "After confirming the job/shoot," he says, "I assemble my wardrobe. Of all the jobs I've done, there has only been one where the wardrobe has been supplied. I often go shopping and try to buy clothes that look like the description of the wardrobe that I've been told to bring."

After Josh arrives for a shoot, he introduces himself, then gives the photographer and the assistant his wardrobe. "I get myself a cup of coffee, take off my glasses, put in my contacts, and wait for them to prepare the set," he says. "It seems like most of the time is spent setting up the lights, the props, and while they are doing that, I usually just sit off to the side waiting. The female models who shoot with me have to have their makeup and hair done, and that also contributes to my waiting-around time." Josh says that he never has makeup applied because it would work against him. "Thanks to an Irish mother and a Filipino father, I have distinguishing characteristics that would be covered by makeup. Freckles on a dark-skinned person have gotten some attention for me thus far. People never know what I am. They think I'm Hispanic, Italian, Mediterranean, or something."

Once all the equipment is set up, lighting tested, and the models are ready, the shoot begins. "A concept or idea of a shoot can be story-boarded in much the same way that a movie is prepared," Josh explains. "I did a shoot for fire-safety awareness, and almost every element that I can think of was planned before the shoot. A shoot can also be planned with only a general idea."

Once the photographer and the client are satisfied with the photographs, the shoot is complete. "I shake hands all around," Josh says, "sign my release paper, and take off."

DO I HAVE WHAT IT TAKES TO BE A MODEL?

Josh says that it is important to be open and friendly to the photographers and assistants during a shoot. "People who keep to themselves might find it hard to be open to strangers who are about to take your picture," he says. "So being a little gregarious and social—but definitely yourself—helps. It's worked for me."

There are significant differences in the requirements necessary for each type of model. The major requirement for the fashion model is, of course, physical appearance. Although most people think of all models as being young and slender, that is not necessarily the case. No set standard exists for a model's physical description because many different body types are needed. Many garment manufacturers seek female fashion models who are between the ages of 16 and 30, between 5 feet 8 inches and 5 feet 11 inches in height and wear from a size 6 to a size 10. Male models generally must be between 6 feet and 6 feet 2 inches in height and wear a size 40 or 42 regular suit. People who fail to meet these specifications, however, should not feel that there are no possibilities for them in this career; after all, garments and other fashion items are made for people of all sizes and types. Also, atypical models who do not necessarily possess classical model features, proportions, or body types, but display interesting or unusual personal style, increasingly are being seen on runways and in photo advertisements, reflecting designer, commercial, and public acceptance of cultural and physical diversity and individual expression in fashion.

Because some fashion houses create styles for people of middle years whose weight is closer to average, more mature looking models sometimes are needed. Other firms that specialize in evening clothes often require models of above average height to display their garments. Companies that produce junior sizes require models who can wear those sizes without alterations. Those that manufacture misses' or women's sizes may seek models who can wear sizes 8, 10, or 12. They also may seek full-figured models who wear sizes 14 or larger. Petite models are 5-feet 5-inches and wear uneven sizes such as three, five, and seven.

The basic requirement for photographers' models is that they photograph well. It must be emphasized, however, that not all attractive people have the qualities that commercial photographers require. Many times characteristics such as wholesomeness and sincerity, as well as freshness of face or manner, are as important in this field as good looks.

Modeling is a particularly fatiguing occupation because it requires many hours of standing and walking, or sitting or standing still in uncomfortable positions. Thus, good health and physical stamina are important. "You need to be in good shape," Josh advises. "My workout is modeled on the Army Ranger workout. The physical fitness test to be a U.S. Army Ranger requires that you be able to do at least six pull-ups, 52 push-ups, 62 sit-ups, and run two miles in under 15 minutes. I do Pilates for extra stomach work and yoga to stay flexible. I don't have to look like a guy in a fitness magazine, but fit."

In addition, those people interested in being fashion or photographic models must be prepared to give up most of their social life and limit their diets. To maintain their figures and appearances, they will require many extra hours of sleep each night and will need to avoid rich foods and beverages. "I eat like a cross between a dog and a pig—anything and quickly," Josh says. "My girlfriend helps keep me in line with not overeating."

Another important requirement is immaculate grooming. Fashion and photographic models will have to spend more hours than the average person taking care of their skin, hair, nails, and general physical fitness. Especially important to fashion models is the ability to walk gracefully while carrying their hands, arms, and torso in a poised and chic manner.

Most fashion and photographers' models must have special training to meet all of the above requirements. Entering a reputable modeling school to learn the skills and techniques of modeling or enrolling in a good charm school to learn makeup application, appropriate clothing, and the proper ways to walk and stand are also helpful and can be a shortcut into the business.

HOW DO I BECOME A MODEL?

Education

High School

There are no standard educational requirements for models. Most employers of photographic models prefer at least a high school education. Courses such as sewing, home economics, and photography are helpful. Classes in dance, fencing, Asian arts such as Tai Chi, and other studies that focus on body and movement control provide a good foundation for modeling. Public speaking and business courses are helpful since models often work as freelancers.

Postsecondary Training

Many employers of models state a preference for college graduates with the ability to communicate well and with a general cultural background. Academic courses may include art, drama, art history, photography, history, English, speech, or debate. Some models take special courses in sports or physical fitness, such as dance, swimming, skiing, skating, aerobics, or horseback riding to get into and stay in shape and develop physical coordination, suppleness, and grace. As models often keep track of their own expenses, a basic knowledge of bookkeeping and mathematics is also helpful.

Internships and Volunteerships

There are no internships available for aspiring models, but you can read about the modeling industry and contact modeling agencies to gain an understanding of what their needs may include. Experience in fashion modeling may be obtained in home economics courses as well as from local fashion shows. Many fashion design schools stage fashion shows for their students' designs and need amateur models to donate their time. You might also volunteer at a fashion firm or related organization to learn more about modeling and other careers in the industry.

WHO WILL HIRE ME?

Josh was encouraged by his girlfriend to reenter the field after an eight-year absence. "She happened to find that Gingiss advertisement I did and asked me about it," he recalls. "She told me that I should pursue modeling again. I dismissed it as if it was a fluke that I got the job in the first place. She kept pestering me until finally I had a photographer take my picture. I sent copies of my picture to about 20 agents, and then I just waited and answered the phone."

The approximately 4,600 models employed in the United States work in a variety of settings that require different skills and qualifications. Fashion models may be employed by apparel firms or retail stores; photographic models work through one or more agencies for a variety of clients. High-fashion models usually work in major fashion centers such as New York, London, or Paris. Large cities generally offer more opportunities for modeling work than small towns.

A large percentage of those in the modeling industry do not work full time as model, since there are far more applicants than assignments. Therefore many models have other means of supporting themselves. Models generally choose part-time jobs, especially those with flexible schedules or evening work, in order to be available for auditions and assignments. Many work as restaurant servers, though individuals with special skills or training may find other work. Some work in sales, which allows them flexibility in schedules and number of hours.

To gain employment as an artist's model, men or women may apply directly at various art schools, cautiously check newspaper want ads, or apply at the state employment office.

Graduates of modeling schools may be aided by school career services offices in securing their first job. Another possibility for the prospective model is to register at a modeling agency. Aspiring models, however, should be wary of disreputable agencies or schools that promise jobs for a fee toward the purchase of a portfolio of photographs or a contract for modeling classes. Legitimate agencies and modeling schools are listed in industry publications. Choose a modeling agency certified by such bodies as the Screen Actors Guild (SAG) or check with your local Better Business Bureau or Chamber of Commerce to make sure the agency or school is licensed by the state education department before signing an agreement or paying money to an agency or service that promises jobs.

Many agencies select only those people with qualities they believe their clients will demand. If accepted by an agency, the future model's composite card and photographs are placed on file and the model will be called for a job when the agency feels they have one for which the person is qualified. In return for the agency's services, models pay 15 to 20 percent of their earnings to the agency.

All models who wish to have a career in modeling are required to have a collection of photographs to show prospective employers. These photographs should include at least one headshot and several full-length shots in various kinds of situations and garments to show the model's versatility and ability to sell whatever he or she is modeling. Photographic models must have multiple copies of these photographs to leave with potential employers. The back of each picture should list the model's name, address, a contact phone number, height, weight, and coloring, along with clothing and shoe sizes. This picture will be placed in a file along with pictures of many other models. When someone of this type and size is needed for a picture, the model may be called to pose. Models include tear sheets in their portfolios from the assignments they have completed. These sheets prove to prospective employers the model's experience and ability.

Aspiring models who plan to seek work in a large, unfamiliar city should go there prepared to look for a job for at least three months. They should have enough money to support themselves and pay for such modeling necessities as a fashionable wardrobe, professional hair and beauty care, adequate diet, and such incidentals as additional photographs or special short-term training.

WHERE CAN I GO FROM HERE?

The modeling profession has no standard line of advancement. It is rare for artists' models to advance in the usual sense of the word. It is to be expected, however, that the better art schools and the more successful artists may pay higher hourly wages to experienced models.

Advancement for fashion or photographic models takes the form of increased income and greater demand for their talent. Their careers, however, are usually short. The model who works in the field for longer than eight years is considered highly unusual. Certain physical changes and lifestyle often make it difficult for older people to compete with younger models for the same type of assignments.

Even a high degree of success can lead to the shortening of a model's career. When models appear too frequently on magazine covers or in features, the uniqueness of their look becomes familiar, and they are passed by in favor of models who have not received such wide coverage. Also, models who become identified with one particular product, such as a line of makeup or shampoo, may find it difficult to qualify for jobs with other employers.

Most fashion and photographic models must therefore learn a marketable skill or profession to which they may turn when they can no longer continue modeling. Many fashion models gain enough knowledge to move into fashion design, advertising, public relations, or retailing. Others attend special schools between modeling assignments to learn business, technical, or vocational skills. Still others go to work for modeling agencies or open agencies of their own. Modeling can be a gateway to consulting jobs in the fashion and merchandising field, and some models serve as board members of fashion magazines. Other models become actors and actresses. Well-known models may develop their own line of cosmetics or other products.

In the future, Josh plans to take acting lessons. "I have no goals regarding acting," he says. "I didn't have any goals about modeling and still don't. I would like to do commercials, and possibly get paid to act. But I think doing community theater would be just fine with me. I suppose the next most logical step would be to do bigger, better-paying jobs, or go to the other side of the camera. I'm learning about this field myself, so I don't really have detailed plans other than staying fit, having fun, and being myself. I hope in 5 to 10 years I'm working on a television show, or at Steppenwolf."

WHAT ARE THE SALARY RANGES?

Earnings for models vary according to experience and depend on the number, length, and type of assignments he or she receives. Today, top fashion models working full-time for wholesalers or retailers earn approximately $40,000 or more a year. Models working retail shows earn between $15,000 and $18,000 or more each year. Female models working for agencies make $100 to $125 an hour. Hourly wages are higher for photographic models working in large metropolitan cities such as New York, Miami, Los Angeles, or Chicago and for models who are in great demand. Top photographic models signed to exclusive contracts with cosmetic firms may earn $1 million or more per year. Almost all models work with agents and pay 15 to 20 percent of their earnings in return for an agent's services.

The U.S. Department of Labor reports that median earnings of models were $20,980 in 2004. The lowest 10 percent earned less than $13,790, and the highest 10 percent earned more than $35,730.

Models who appear in television commercials are paid according to the fee schedules set up by the two major unions, the Screen Actors Guild (SAG) and the American Federation of Television and Radio Artists (AFTRA). Models who speak earn more than those who do not. In addition, they receive a fee called a residual whenever the commercial is aired.

Fashion models who are employed by department stores are called *floor models.* They work only for special promotions at the store and earn the same salary as salespeople. The rate of pay is generally between $8 and $12 an hour, depending on the size and location of the store and the quality and cost of the merchandise. Models who work for advertising agencies may earn between $15 and $25 an hour. The more versatile the model, the greater the opportunity for employment.

Because they are seldom employed full time, instead earning a high hourly fee on an occasional basis, photographic models may not always have enough money to maintain themselves between jobs. They may find it necessary to seek other kinds of work on a temporary basis. It is essential that they have outstanding wardrobes, so they frequently work at part-time jobs to buy the necessary clothes for their assignments. Models occasionally receive clothing or clothing discounts instead of, or in addition to, regular earnings.

The only full-time employment for models usually is as a spokesperson for a store or company. Full-time models usually receive up to two or three weeks of vacation per year. The perks of being a fashion model include the chance to wear beautiful clothes, look your best, and be groomed by photographers, designers, artists, and hair and makeup professionals. Some models travel to exciting places and meet interesting and famous people; a very few may even attain celebrity status. Indeed, today's fashion and cosmetics supermodels have achieved a celebrity status that formerly was the exclusive domain of movie stars. Historically, the industry favors youth, but agencies are now using older models more often and the age barrier seems to be coming down. Young people who hope to become models, however, should approach the career with the understanding that competition is keen and that it may take years of work to attain success. But even the beginner, on a local level, can make enough money to make this career worthwhile.

Related Jobs

- actors
- cosmetologists
- fashion coordinators
- fashion designers
- fashion illustrators and photographers
- fashion model agents
- fashion stylists
- film and television extras
- makeup artists
- photographers
- product demonstrators
- product promoters
- talent agents and scouts

WHAT IS THE JOB OUTLOOK?

The U.S. Department of Labor predicts employment for models to grow about as fast as the average through 2014, but job competition will be fierce because this career is attractive to so many people. The number of fashion models seeking jobs is far greater than the number of openings. A greater number of openings exist for artists' models, but their income almost never is enough to live on. Part-time work is easier to find than full-time work. The number of models working should increase as the economy becomes more global. Models from the United States are in demand around the world. Opportunities for male models should also increase as the public becomes more open to the marketing of men's fashions. Most openings will occur as models quit or retire to pursue other employment or interests.

SECTION 3

Do It Yourself

"What are you going to do with your life?" Your friends and family have probably asked you that question countless times. Since you are reading this book, it is obvious that you are interested in fashion, but are you aware of all the career options available to you (and the ways to learn more about them)? When most people think of fashion careers, they think of designers busily creating the latest fashions and models strutting down the catwalk flaunting these creations before throngs of industry professionals. But did you know there are countless other opportunities available to young people with an interest in fashion? If you have business acumen, there are opportunities to be buyers, advertising and marketing workers, agents, and managers. In addition to fashion design, those with creative ability can work as makeup artists, illustrators, photographers, and stylists. For those who have a way with words, there are opportunities with magazines, book publishers, and newspapers. And for those who are more technically adept, there are jobs in manufacturing. In short, opportunities in fashion are only limited by your imagination!

No matter what career you're interested in, you are probably already sketching out designs, watching television shows about fashion, or perhaps even looking into modeling. That's a great start, but not the only way to learn more about fashion careers. You probably have never stopped to think of all the different ways you can learn more about fashion careers while you are still in high school. The following section provides tips on how to learn more about fashion through hands-on experience. After reading through these suggestions, chances are you'll think of even more ways to learn about fashion. The key is to get cracking now while you're in high school, so that you'll be ready to enter the field or pursue a college education in fashion after you graduate.

Read! Read! Read!

So you want to work in the fashion industry? There's more to it than knowing which shoes go with which outfit. Arm yourself with knowledge—and what better way than by reading industry "bibles" such as *Women's Wear Daily* (http://www.wwd.com), *Vogue* (http://www.style.com/vogue), and *Glamour* (http://www.glamour.com). Not only will you learn the latest styles coming off the runways, you'll also be acquainted with up-and-coming designers and their products. Many of these magazines also offer online versions or publish separate monthly issues targeted specifically to the teen audience. Titles such as *ELLEgirl* (http://www.ellegirl.com) and *CosmoGirl* (http://www.cosmogirl.com) carry fashion information similar to their big sister magazines, but also offer editorial content, trends, and advertising more suited to the younger reader. Some magazines, such as *ELLEgirl,* have teenaged contributors on their editorial staff. *CosmoGirl* keeps a Style Council composed of high school students to give their opinions on new trends in fashion. This route may be of interest, especially if you are considering fashion reporting as a possible career.

Women's Wear Daily, a Fairchild publication, also has a sister monthly simply titled *W* (http://www.style.com/w). Also, you many want to check out other Fairchild publications that cover other fashion trades you may not have considered, such as footwear, children's wear, and men's wear. Visit http://www.fairchildpub.com/index.cfm for more information.

Your local library holds a wealth of information on the history of fashion. Learn when and how clothing evolved from a simple necessity to a multi-billion dollar industry. It's important to recognize today's hot designers, but even more impressive to know early Parisian houses of fashion such as Chanel and Worth. So read up and know the difference between haute couture and prêt a porter! (For more information on books and other publications, see the "Read a Book" section.)

Get a Job!

A part-time job will not only fill your resume with relevant work experience, it will also pad your wallet! You may want to start at your favorite clothing store. Many retail chains hire high school students and even cater to their school schedules. Sales associates do more than sell clothes—they are responsible for merchandise displays, promotions, and consultations. That's a career's worth of work experience in one job! If hair and makeup is more your interest, apply to neighborhood beauty salons. Your entry-level position could be as a receptionist, shampoo person, or makeup assistant.

Unless you are actually under contract as a model, part-time work at a modeling agency can be harder to get. The biggest hurdle is location. Almost all large modeling agencies are based in New York, though some may have satellite offices in other cities. Try looking in your town's phone book, or surf the Web for modeling agencies in your area. Though they may be smaller in size and clientele, such agencies may be sources of some sort of part-time employment. You may be asked to help with the front desk, or work as a photographer's or booker's assistant.

Take Classes

Education is important, but in this industry so is talent. Hone your skills and creativity by taking as many classes as possible. Are you hoping to get into fashion design? Then enroll in sewing, drawing, and computer design classes. Is makeup design your interest? Why not take classes in proper makeup application or nail art techniques? Check with a beauty school for classes in hairstyling and design. Do you aspire to be the next Annie Liebowitz or Francesco Scavullo? A good photography class is the first step to realizing your dream. Not only will you learn the key to taking great fashion photos, you'll also learn the importance of a good portfolio, and whether or not to use a photo agent. Log on to http://www.fashion.net/howto/photography for more tips on breaking into this exciting career.

It's not your mother's home economics class. Luckily, many high schools now offer fashion design classes as electives, some as early as the freshman level. At Carl Sandburg High School in Orland Park, Illinois, students learn about patterns, fabrics, and the basics of sewing. Projects such as a purse and slacks are part of the final grade. At Herndon High School in Herndon, Virginia, fashion merchandising and marketing are just some topics that are studied. Students enrolled in the fashion program also take an annual trip to New York City, the nation's fashion mecca.

If your school does not offer such classes, don't despair. Turn to your town's park district or community college, where many fashion, sewing, knitting, and photography classes are offered. Fabric stores are also good sources for classes in sewing and pattern cutting/fitting.

Be Your Own Boss

Okay—you've taken the classes, are you ready to set up shop? Absolutely! If your friends and family love the jeans you've embellished, or beg you to make uniquely beaded necklaces, it's time to do so for profit. Get a good inventory together, and hit the flea markets, art fairs, or target your classmates at school. Don't forget to name your business, and market yourself properly—with flyers and business cards. Wear your creations, or get your friends to model them for you at school, dances, and other activities. There's nothing like free advertising!

Don't limit your business to apparel. Are you good at styling hair or applying makeup? Then make your services known at school—especially during prom season. Create a flyer describing your services and their cost. Gauge how much area salons are charging for such services and set your prices well below—girls are always going to be looking for a bargain! Other services that people are willing to pay for are shopping, decorating, or organizing wardrobes. If you have a flair for putting together the right outfit, or finding the perfect gift, you are sitting on a talent gold mine!

One thing to consider is that some people may need your services but may not be able to pay. Don't fret. Find out what talents your friends have to offer, and trade your services for theirs. Bartering is quite common in the fashion industry. Does your friend make beautiful knitted hats? Offer a free wardrobe consultation in exchange!

Plan a Fashion Show

Fashion shows are always glamorous and exciting affairs to attend—but the real work takes place on the other side of the runway curtain. Think you have what it takes to be a fashion show coordinator? Why not organize a fashion show benefiting your school, organization, or favorite charity? You'll need to find a venue; recruit models, hairstylists, and makeup artists; pick a theme; and secure clothing from designers or area stores—just to start. As coordinator you can delegate some of the duties, but ultimately the responsibility for the final product rests on your shoulders.

Join or Start a Fashion Club

Join your high school's fashion club and meet other fashionistas! It's a great forum in which to discuss fashion, designing, shopping, and modeling. Perhaps your club can offer lectures from modeling agents on the different types of modeling careers available. Or raise funds by selling jewelry and other accessories handmade by club members. Or photograph and style a school calendar using fellow students as models. If your school does not have a fashion club, then step up to the plate and be the founding member. You'll first have to get your principal's permission as well as find a teacher willing to serve as the club's moderator. Next, pick a name and advertise scheduled projects—your club is sure to be a hit! For more suggestions on starting a fashion club, log on to http://www.fashionclub.com.

Volunteer or Do Contract Work

Sometimes the best jobs in fashion may provide great experience, but not great pay. You may be able to volunteer at fashion shows or bridal shows doing anything from setting up chairs and backdrops to buttoning up a model bride's bustle. It may not pay well, but at least you'll see the behind-the-scenes action of a real show. Call modeling agencies or bridal salons in your area to offer your services.

Some jobs are also filled on a contract basis. For example, a modeling agency will hire employees on a project-to-project basis. Contract employees may be sent to different cities in the United States to work at model searches. They may be responsible for processing applications, shooting Polaroids of model candidates, or assembling marketing kits. Though contract employees are given straight pay without benefits, they receive travel expenses and other perks. More importantly, it's a foot in the company's door, and a chance to make industry contacts. Many contract employees are hired permanently after making a good impression with the boss.

Visit Museum Exhibits and Fashion Shows

Learn the industry's history by attending exhibits at museums and schools. Today, fashion is considered by some to be an art form—having the same elements of design and beauty as painting or sculpture. The Museum of Science & Industry in Chicago and New York's Metropolitan Museum of Modern Art, among many others, have hosted traveling exhibits of famous designers such as Gianni Versace and Andy Warhol, Princess Diana's dress collection, and jewelry collections of royal families. Exhibits are constantly changing—your best bet is to periodically check your museum's Web page to learn of upcoming exhibits. Also, read the style section of your local newspaper to learn where such exhibits are held.

Attend fashion shows. Fashion shows are where designers showcase new collections for the upcoming season. There are fashion shows that focus on showcasing women's clothing, as well as men's and children's wear. Some shows are even devoted to footwear. You may wish to attend a glamorous fashion show during New York's Fashion Week, but those seats are pretty hard to snag. There are other alternatives. Area retail stores often hold smaller fashion shows to promote new clothing lines they are carrying. There may be a small entrance fee, but usually attendees are given a goodie bag of merchandise or discount card for future purchases. Marshall Field's, a Chicago retail giant, holds an annual Glamorama gala, which showcases the store's well-known names, as well as emerging designers. For more information, visit http://www.factiomagazine.com/specialfeatures/spe__Glamorama2005.htm.

Design schools such as the School of the Art Institute of Chicago (http://www.artic.edu/saic) and the Fashion Institute of Technology (http://www.fitnyc.edu/html/dynamic.html) in New York also hold fashion shows to promote the work of their graduating classes.

Who Doesn't Love a Winner?

There are a variety of fashion contests looking for the best design, concept, or essay. The prizes are outstanding and can range from designer merchandise to personal makeovers to free trips to fashion capitals in the United States. The biggest prize, of course, is the experience you'll gain from such contests . . . and winner's bragging rights! Many contests are open to high school students. The Internet is a good place to find out about contests—check out the Fashion Club Web site (http://www.fashionclub.com/perks-and-prizes/contests/contests-prizes.shtm) for a list of upcoming contests and past winners' loot. Also turn to fashion magazines and fashion schools for upcoming design contests. The Illinois Institute of Art–Chicago, along with *ELLEgirl,* sponsors a fashion competition for high school seniors in the United States and Canada. Winners in the fields of fashion design and fashion marketing and merchandising are awarded full scholarships to the school as well as admittance to the top shows during New York's Fashion Week. For more information, visit http://www.ilic.artinstitutes.edu/news_detail.asp?nid=3626. (See the Get Involved section for more information on competitions.)

Job Shadow or Interview an Industry Veteran

Another good way to learn about the fashion industry is to interview someone already in the field. What are some good questions to ask? Anything and everything! Is the job hard? What are the hours? What is the average day like? Special tasks? What are some of the highs and lows of the job? It's your time to learn what it is like to be a coordinator, stylist, fit model, or any other career in the fashion industry. Prepare your questions carefully; writing them down will help you stay organized. Keep to the topic at hand. It's important to dress fashionably, but also neat and tastefully. Only take up as much time as arranged—these people are working, after all!

Job shadowing is like an interview, but more intensive. You'll live a day in the working life of someone in the fashion industry. If you are job shadowing a fashion photographer, you'll follow him or her to fashion shoots and help set up lighting and backdrops. Perhaps you will be able to watch this professional photograph an important ad campaign or shoot composition shots for aspiring models. Job shadowing is a great way to learn about a job because you will be able to live it (at least for a few hours) and make your own impression.

Ask your school guidance or career counselor to help you find possible candidates to interview or job shadow. Or you may want to do your own research and call a company you are particularly interested in. Identify yourself and the purpose of your interview. Good luck! For more information on job shadowing, visit http://www.jobshadow.org/.

SECTION 4

What Can I Do Right Now?

Get Involved

Now that you've read about some of the different careers available in fashion, you may be anxious to experience this line of work for yourself, to find out what it's really like. Or perhaps you already feel certain that this is the career path for you and want to get started on it right away. Whichever is the case, this section is for you! There are plenty of things you can do right now to learn about fashion careers while gaining valuable experience. Just as important, you'll get to meet new friends and see new places, too.

In the following pages you will find programs designed to pique your interest in fashion and start preparing you for a career. You already know that there are a wide variety of options available, and that to work in it you need a solid education and, for many careers, well-developed creative skills. Since the first step toward a fashion career will be gaining that education, we've found more than 30 programs that will start you on your way. Some are special introductory sessions, others are actual college courses—one of them may be right for you. Take time to read the listings and see how each compares to your situation: how committed you are to fashion, how much of your money and free time you're willing to devote to it, and how the program will help you after high school. These listings are divided into categories, with the type of program printed right after its name or the name of the sponsoring organization.

❑ THE CATEGORIES

Camps

When you see an activity that is classified as a camp, don't automatically start packing your tent and mosquito repellent. Where academic study is involved, the term "camp" often simply means a residential program including both educational and recreational activities. It's sometimes hard to differentiate between such camps and other study programs, but if the sponsoring organization calls it a camp, so do we!

College Courses/Summer Study

These terms are linked because most college courses offered to students your age must take place in the summer, when you are out of school. At the same time, colleges and universities that want to attract future students and give them a head start in higher education sponsor many summer study programs. Summer study of almost any type is a good idea because it keeps your mind and your study skills sharp over the long vacation. Summer study at a college offers any number of additional benefits, including giving you the tools to make a well-informed decision about your future academic career.

Competitions

Competitions are fairly self-explanatory, but you should know that there are only a few in this book for the following reason: many fashion competitions are at the local and regional levels and are impractical to list here. What this means, however, is that if you are interested in entering a competition, you shouldn't have much trouble finding one yourself. Your guidance counselor or family and consumer science teacher can help you start searching in your area.

Conferences

Conferences for high school students are usually difficult to track down because most are for professionals in the field who gather to share new information and ideas with each other. Don't be discouraged, though. A number of professional organizations with student branches invite those student members to their conferences and plan special events for them. Some student branches even run their own conferences; check the directory of organizations at the end of this section for possible leads. This is an option worth pursuing because conferences focus on some of the most current information available and also give you the chance to meet professionals who can answer your questions and even offer advice.

Employment and Internship Opportunities

As you may already know from experience, employment opportunities for teenagers can be very limited. Even internships are most often reserved for college students who have completed at least one or two years of study in the field. Still, if you're very determined to find an internship or paid position in fashion, there may be ways to find one. See the "Do It Yourself" section in this book for some suggestions.

Field Experience

This is something of a catchall category for activities that don't exactly fit the other descriptions. But anything called a field experience in this book is always a good opportunity to get out and explore the work of fashion professionals.

Membership

When an organization is in this category, it simply means that you are welcome to pay your dues and become a card-carrying member. Formally joining any organization brings the benefits of meeting others who share your interests, finding opportunities to get involved, and keeping up with current events. Depending on how active you are, the contacts you make and the experiences you gain may help when the time comes to apply to colleges or look for a job.

In some organizations, you pay a special student rate and receive benefits similar to regular members. Many organizations, however, are now starting student branches with their own benefits and publications. As in any field, make sure you understand exactly what the benefits of membership are before you join.

Finally, don't let membership dues discourage you from making contact with these organizations. Some charge dues as low as $10 because they know that students are perpetually short of funds. When the annual dues are higher, think of the money as an investment in your future and then consider if it is too much to pay.

❑ PROGRAM DESCRIPTIONS

Once you've started to look at the individual listings themselves, you'll find that they contain a lot of information. Naturally, there is a general description of each program, but wherever possible we also have included the following details.

Application Information

Once you have determined the application deadline for participating in a specific opportunity, apply for the program or position as far in advance as possible. This ensures that you won't miss out on a great opportunity simply because other people got there ahead of you. It also means that you will get a timely decision on your application, so if you are not accepted, you'll still have some time to apply elsewhere. As for the things that make up your application—essays, portfolio, recommendations, etc.—we've tried to cover what's involved, but be sure to contact the program about specific requirements before you submit anything.

Background Information

This includes such information as the date, the name of the organization that is sponsoring it financially, and the faculty and staff who will be there for you. This can help you—and your family—gauge the quality and reliability of the program.

Classes and Activities

Classes and activities change from year to year, depending on popularity, availability of instructors, and many other factors. Nevertheless, colleges and universities quite consistently offer the same or similar classes, even in their summer sessions. Courses like "Introduction to Fashion Design," for example, are simply indispensable. So you can look through the listings and see which programs offer foundational courses like this and which offer courses on more variable topics. As for activities, we note when you have access to recreational facilities on campus, and it's usually a given that special social and cultural activities will be arranged for most programs.

Contact Information

Wherever possible, we have given the title of the person whom you should contact instead of the name because people change jobs so frequently. If no title is given and you are telephoning an organization, simply tell the person who answers the phone the name of the program that interests you and he or she will forward your call. If you are writing, include the line "Attention: Summer Study Program" (or whatever is appropriate after "Attention") somewhere on the envelope. This will help to ensure that your letter goes to the person in charge of that program.

Credit

Where academic programs are concerned, we sometimes note that high school or college credit is available to those who have completed them. This means that the program can count toward your high school diploma or a future college degree just like a regular course. Obviously, this can be very useful, but it's important to note that rules about accepting such credit vary from school to school. Before you commit to a program offering high school credit, check with your guidance counselor to see if it is acceptable to your school. As for programs offering college credit, check with your chosen college (if you have one) to see if they will accept it.

Eligibility and Qualifications

The main eligibility requirement to be concerned about is age or grade in school. A term frequently used in relation to grade level is "rising," as in "rising senior": someone who will be a senior when the next school year begins. This is especially important where summer programs are concerned. A number of university-based programs make admissions decisions partly in consideration of GPA, class rank, and standardized test scores. This is mentioned in the listings, but you must contact the program for specific numbers. If you are worried that your GPA or your ACT scores, for example, aren't good enough, don't let them stop you from applying to programs that consider such things in the admissions process. Often, a fine essay or even an example of your dedication and eagerness can compensate for statistical weaknesses.

Facilities

We tell you where you'll be living, studying, eating, and having fun during these programs, but there isn't enough room to go into all the details. Some of those details can be important: what is and isn't accessible for people with disabilities, whether the site of a summer program has air-conditioning, and how modern the studios and computer equipment are. You can expect most program brochures and application materials to address these concerns, but if you still have questions about the facilities, just call the program's administration and ask.

Financial Details

While a few of the programs listed here are fully underwritten by collegiate and corporate sponsors, most of them rely on you for at least some of their funding. The 2005 prices and fees are given here, but you should bear in mind that costs rise slightly almost every year. You and your parents must take costs into consideration when choosing a program. We always try to note where financial aid is available, but really, most programs will do their best to ensure that a shortage of funds does not prevent you from taking part.

Residential Versus Commuter Options

Simply put, some programs prefer that participating students live with other participants and staff members, others do not, and still others leave the decision entirely to the students themselves. As a rule, residential programs are suitable for young people who live out of town or even out of state, as well as for local residents. They generally provide a better overview of college life than programs in which you're only on campus for a few hours a day, and they're a way to test how well you cope with living away from home. Commuter programs may be viable only if you live near the program site or if you can stay with relatives who do. Bear in mind that for residential programs especially, the travel between your home and the location of the activity is almost always your responsibility and can significantly increase the cost of participation.

Finally . . .

Ultimately, there are three important things to bear in mind concerning all of the programs listed in this volume. The first is that things change. Staff members come and go, funding is added or withdrawn, supply and demand determine which programs continue and which terminate. Dates, times, and costs vary widely due to a number of factors. Because of this, the information we give you, although as current and detailed as possible, is just not enough on which to base your final decision. If you are interested in a program, you simply must write, call, fax, or e-mail the organization concerned to get the latest and most complete information available. This has the added benefit of putting you in touch with someone who can deal with your individual questions and problems.

Another important point to keep in mind when considering these programs is that the people who run them provided the information printed here. The editors of this book haven't attended the programs and don't endorse them: we simply give you the information with which to begin your own research. And after all, we can't pass judgment because you're the only one who can decide which programs are right for you.

The final thing to bear in mind is that the programs listed here are just the tip of the iceberg. No book can possibly cover all of the opportunities that are available to you—partly because they are so numerous and are constantly coming and going, and partly because some are waiting to be discovered. For instance, you may be very interested in taking a college course but don't see the college that interests you in the listings. Call their Admissions Office! Even if they don't have a special program for high school students, they might be able to make some kind of arrangements for you to visit or sit in on a class. Use the ideas behind these listings and take the initiative to turn them into opportunities!

❑ THE PROGRAMS

Academic Study Associates

College Courses/Summer Study

Academic Study Associates has been offering residential and commuter pre-college summer programs for young people for more than 20 years. It offers college credit classes and enrichment opportunities in a variety of academic fields, including drawing, photography, graphic design, and creative writing, at the University of Massachusetts-Amherst, the University of California-Berkeley, Emory University, and Oxford University (in the United Kingdom). In addition to classroom/studio work, students participate in field trips, mini-clinics, and extracurricular activities. Programs are usually three to four weeks in length. Fees and deadlines vary for these programs—visit the ASA Web site for further details. Options are also available for middle school students.

Academic Study Associates (ASA)
ASA Programs
375 West Broadway, Suite 200
New York, NY 10012-4324
800-752-2250
summer@asaprograms.com
http://www.asaprograms.com/home/asa_home.asp

American Collegiate Adventures (ACA)

College Courses/Summer Study

American Collegiate Adventures offers high school students the chance to experience and prepare for college during their summer vacation. Adventures are based at the University of Wisconsin in Madison; they vary in length from three to six weeks. Participants attend college-level courses (available for credit or as a noncredit enrichment option) taught by university faculty during the week and visit regional colleges and recreation sites over the weekend. All students live in comfortable (suite) accommodations, just down the hall from an ACA resident staff member. Courses vary but usually include such basics as "Fashion Design," "Drawing and Painting," "Photography," and "Creative Writing"—perfect for those planning to pursue a degree in fashion. Programs in Italy and Spain are also available. Contact American Collegiate Adventures for the current course listings, prices, and application procedures.

American Collegiate Adventures
1811 West North Avenue, Suite 201
Chicago, IL 60622-0202
800-509-7867
info@acasummer.com
http://www.zfc-consulting.com/webprojects/americanadventures

The Arts! At Maryland

College Courses/Summer Study

The Arts! At Maryland Program is sponsored by the University of Maryland for motivated juniors and seniors who are interested in visual arts, writing, and other fields. Participants in the three-week program spend July exploring the field of visual arts and taking a college-level course—such as "Drawing I." Students spend time in the studio, the classroom, and on field trips to galleries and studios. College credit is awarded to students who satisfactorily complete the course. Participants can commute or live in the residence halls at the University of Maryland and take their meals on campus or in selected College Park restaurants. To apply, you must submit an application form, an essay, two letters of recommendation, a current transcript, and an application fee by mid-May. Admissions decisions are based primarily on recommendations and overall academic ability. For further details (including information on cost of tuition) and an application form, visit the Web site listed below or contact the Summer Sessions and Special Programs staff.

Summer Sessions and Special Programs
Mitchell Building, 1st Floor
University of Maryland
College Park, MD 20742-0001
877-989-7762
http://www.summer.umd.edu/c/admissions/courses/taam

Camp Ballibay

Camps

Camp Ballibay, established in 1964, is accredited by the American Camping Association. It offers programs (two to nine weeks in length) in visual arts, photography, theater, vocal and instrumental music, ballet, modern jazz and tap dance, video, radio, and technical theater for students ages 6 to 16. In addition to classes, students participate in various extracurricular activities. Campers stay in cabins and have access to art studios, a swimming pool, a riding area, tennis courts, sports fields, an infirmary, a camp store, and a dining hall. Tuition for this residential camp ranges from $1,950 to $6,250 depending on the length of the program. Contact Camp Ballibay for further information.

Camp Ballibay
One Ballibay Road
Camptown, PA 18815
570-746-3233
jannone@ballibay.com
http://www.ballibay.com

College and Careers Program at the Rochester Institute of Technology

College Courses/Summer Study

The Rochester Institute of Technology (RIT) offers its College and Careers Program for rising high school seniors who want to experience college life and explore career options in a variety of subject areas. The program, founded in 1990, allows you to spend a Friday and Saturday on campus, living in the dorms and attending four sessions on the career areas of your choice. Past fashion industry–related sections included "Marketing: Will Your Idea Sell?," "Illustration," and "Photography." In each session, participants work with RIT students and faculty to gain hands-on experience in the subject area. This residential program is held twice each summer, usually once in mid-July and again in early August. The registration deadline is one week before the start of the program, but space is limited and students are accepted on a first-come, first-served basis. For further information about the program and specific sessions on offer, contact the RIT admissions office.

College and Careers Program
Rochester Institute of Technology
Office of Admissions
60 Lomb Memorial Drive
Rochester, NY 14623-5604

585-475-6631
http://www.rit.edu/~960www/careers2005/index.php3

Council of Fashion Designers of America

Employment and Internship Opportunities, Field Experience

The council offers several useful programs for college fashion students and young professionals. Graduating college seniors who have pursued education in fashion design may apply for a one-year, paid internship via the Target/CFDA Design Initiative. Interns work with designers or at design or major retail companies. The Professional Development Program for young fashion professionals offers seminars/workshops on fashion-related topics. The Visiting Designers program allows undergraduate students to talk with designers and have their work critiqued.

Council of Fashion Designers of America
1412 Broadway, Suite 2006
New York, NY 10018-9250
212-302-1821
info@cfda.com
http://www.cfda.com

Exploration Summer Programs (ESP) at Yale University

College Courses/Summer Study

Exploration Summer Programs has been offering academic summer enrichment programs to students for nearly 30 years. Rising high school sophomores, juniors, and seniors can participate in ESP's Senior Program at Yale University. Two, three-week residential and day sessions are available and are typically held in June and July. Participants can choose from more than 80 courses. Recent courses included "From Rags to Runway: Fashion Redesign," "Shutterbug: Photography," "From Sketches to Still Life: Drawing," "Stop the Presses!: Journalism," and "Can You Hear Me Now?: Advertising + Marketing." Students entering the 11th or 12th grades can take college seminars, which provide course work that is similar to that of first-year college study. All courses and seminars are ungraded and not-for-credit. In addition to academics, students participate in extracurricular activities such as tours, sports, concerts, weekend recreational trips, college trips, and discussions of current events and other issues. Tuition for the Residential Senior Program is approximately $4,100 for one session and $7,400 for two sessions. Day session tuition ranges from approximately $2,100 for one session to $3,795 for two sessions. A limited number of need-based partial and full scholarships are available. Programs are also available for students in grades four through nine. Contact ESP for more information.

Exploration Summer Programs
470 Washington Street, PO Box 368
Norwood, MA 02062-0368
781-762-7400
http://www.explo.org

Fashion and Clothing Camp

Camps

Students in Tennessee who are entering grades 7 through 12 can participate in a three-day residential Fashion and Clothing Camp. Camps are sponsored by the Tennessee State 4-H Office, and are held at state universities and other locations throughout Tennessee. Camp participants take field trips and learn more about clothes, fashion, and related topics via discovery activities (there are no lectures). Each camp concludes with a fashion show. Campers receive lodging, meals, workshop materials, and transportation. The cost of this program ranges from approximately $70 to $75. Contact the Tennessee State 4-H Office for more information.

Tennessee State 4-H Office
2621 Morgan Circle, 205 Morgan Hall
Knoxville, TN 37996-4510
865-974-2128
ssutton2@utk.edu
http://4h.tennessee.edu/centersandcamping/specialtycamps.htm

Fashion Camp at the University of South Carolina

Camps

Rising 6th through 12th graders can participate in a weeklong, residential summer Fashion Camp. Campers participate in lessons/activities on color trends, fabric draping, fashion show production, upcoming season predictions, and fashion dos and don'ts. At the end of the week, campers participate in a fashion show. Contact the Fashion Camp coordinator for information on costs and eligibility requirements.

University of South Carolina
College of Hospitality, Retail, & Sport Management
Department of Retailing
Attn: Fashion Camp Coordinator
Carolina Coliseum, Room 2014
Columbia, SC 29208-0001
http://www.hrsm.sc.edu/retail

Fashion Group International, Inc.

Competitions, Conferences, Membership

Fashion Group International, a nonprofit association of more than 6,000 professionals in the fashion, apparel, accessories, beauty, and home industries, offers a career day conference, "Dare to Design Your Future," to college fashion students. Held each fall in New York City, the career day features a seminar program, a design competition that provides awards of $2,500 each in six disciplines, and a job fair for students enrolled at accredited colleges, universities, or chartered schools of design. The organization's regional chapters also offer membership to college students enrolled in fashion-related programs. Contact Fashion Group International for more information.

Fashion Group International, Inc.
8 West 40th Street, 7th Floor
New York, NY 10018-3902
212-302-5511
info@fgi.org
http://www.fgi.org

Global Experiences

College Courses/Summer Study, Employment and Internship Opportunities, Field Experience

Global Experiences "promotes cultural exchange opportunities for individuals wanting to live, work and travel abroad." It offers three fashion-related programs for students: Fashion Internships, Fashion in the Classroom, and Fashion Tours. Students in the Fashion Internships program can learn about global fashion by working as interns in Italy or Australia. Programs last anywhere from 2 to 12 months. Applicants can choose internships in the following areas: fashion design, fashion merchandising, fashion marketing, fashion business administration, and fashion retail. Participants stay together in a shared apartment, although other options—such as single stay, homestay, or studios—are also available for an additional fee. The Fashion in the Classroom program offers students the opportunity to take course work and academic programs in fashion design, fashion merchandising, and fashion business in foreign countries. Fashion Tours allow participants to visit famous fashion cities, tour top fashion houses, and meet industry professionals in a variety of international locales. Costs and program lengths vary by program and location; contact Global Experiences for complete details.

Global Experiences
1010 Pendleton Street
Alexandria, VA 22314-1837
877-432-2762
fashion@globalexperiences.com
http://www.globalexperiences.com

High School Honors Program/ Summer Challenge Program at Boston University

College Courses/Summer Study

Two summer educational opportunities are available for high school students interested in fashion and other majors. Rising high school seniors can participate in the High School Honors Program, which offers six-week, for-credit undergraduate study at the University. Students take two for-credit classes (up to eight credits) alongside regular Boston College students, live in dorms on campus, and participate in extracurricular activities and tours of local attractions. Courses are available in a variety of areas, including advertising, drawing, photography, creative writing, and marketing. The program typically begins in early July. Students who demonstrate financial need may be eligible for financial aid. Tuition for the program is approximately $3,550, with registration/program fees ($350) and room and board options ($1,598 to $1,718) extra. Rising high school sophomores, juniors, and seniors in the University's Summer Challenge Program learn about college life and take college classes in a noncredit setting. The program lasts two weeks and is offered in three sessions. Students get to choose two seminars (which feature lectures, group and individual work, project-based assignments, and field trips) from a total of eight available programs. Seminar choices include visual arts, creative writing, persuasive writing, business, law, international politics, psychology, and science.

Students live in dorms on campus and participate in extracurricular activities and tours of local attractions. The cost of the program is approximately $2,550 (which includes tuition, a room charge, meals, and sponsored activities). Visit the University's Summer Programs Web site for more information.

Boston University Summer Programs
755 Commonwealth Avenue
Boston, MA 02215-1401
617-353-5124
summer@bu.edu
http://www.bu.edu/summer/highschool

High School Summer Institute at Columbia College Chicago

College Courses/Summer Study

Rising high school sophomores, juniors, and seniors can take courses in one of 18 academic areas for college credit via Columbia's five-week High School Summer Institute. Recent classes included "Fundamentals of Fashion Design," "Chicago Fashion Industry," "Introduction to Photography," "Digital Photography," and "Introduction to Marketing Communication." Students stay in residence halls on campus; the approximately $1,400 room-and-board fee includes housing, an evening meal each day, and evening and weekend activities. Tuition is $150 per credit hour; there may be an additional charge for books and other materials. A limited number of scholarships are available. Contact the institute for further details.

High School Summer Institute
Columbia College Chicago
600 South Michigan Avenue
Chicago, IL 60605-1900
312-344-7130
summerinstitute@colum.edu
http://www.colum.edu/admissions/hs_institute

Idyllwild Arts Academy Summer Program

Camps

Since 1950, the Idyllwild Arts Academy has been offering students intensive opportunities to explore the arts. The academy's Youth Arts Center offers a variety of art programs for students between ages 13 and 18, including "Black and White Photography," "Photo Explorations," "Youth Jewelry Workshop," and "Drawing and Painting." Commuter and resident options are available. Most sessions last two weeks, but the Drawing and Painting Program consists of three two-week sessions. Contact the program for information on tuition and fees for room and board. Scholarships are available and are awarded on the basis of financial need and the artistic ability of the applicant.

Idyllwild Arts Academy Summer Program
52500 Temecula Drive
PO Box 38
Idyllwild, CA 92549-0038
951-659-2171, ext. 2223
http://www.idyllwildarts.org/html/summer/summer_programs.html

Interlochen Arts Camp

Camps

Interlochen, located near scenic Traverse City, Michigan, is one of the premier art camps in the United States for young visual artists, musicians, dancers, actors, and writers. High school students can participate in a variety of three- or six-week programs, including "Fibers and Fashion," "Drawing," "Advanced Drawing," "Creative Writing," and "Photography." They can also participate in more than 50 installations, exhibitions, and performance works on campus. Students stay in cabins with 10 to 18 other students and counselors and have access to a private beach, tennis courts, division headquarters, and laundry (students are required to do their own laundry). Extracurricular activities include concerts by well-known musicians, dances, viewing gallery exhibits, arts and crafts, sports, and outdoor activities. The tuition for this camp varies ($3,300 or $5,540 or $5,582) by program, but includes classes, room and board, group instruction, required private lessons, use of all recreational facilities, and admission to student and faculty and performances. Financial aid is available based on the financial need and the artistic ability of the applicant. Programs are also available for students in grades three through eight. Applications for all programs are due in February. Contact the camp for more information.

Interlochen Arts Camp
Admissions Office
PO Box 199
Interlochen, MI 49643-0199
231-276-7472
admissions@interlochen.org
http://www.interlochen.org/camp/cpVa.htm

Intern Exchange International Ltd.

Employment and Internship Opportunities

High school students ages 16 to 18 (including graduating seniors) who are interested in gaining real-life experience in fashion and other areas can participate in month-long internships via Interns Exchange International's Career-Plus Programme in London, England. In classes, participants will learn about fashion- and design-related topics such as fabrics, silhouettes, pattern cutting, trend forecasting, fashion illustration, the role of the designer, and the business of fashion. They also take field trips to the Fashion and Textile Museum and the Victoria & Albert Museum. The cost of the program is approximately $6,200 plus airfare; this fee includes tuition, housing (students live in residence halls at the University of London), breakfast and dinner daily, housekeeping service, linens and towels, special dinner events, weekend trips and excursions, group activities including scheduled theatre, and a Tube Pass. (Note: A Career-Plus Programme is also available in Photography.) Contact the Intern Exchange Director for more information.

Intern Exchange International Ltd.
Attn: Intern Exchange Director
2606 Bridgewood Circle
Boca Raton, FL 33434-4118

561-477-2434
info@internexchange.com
http://www.internexchange.com

International Modeling and Talent Association

Competitions

The International Modeling and Talent Association, an organization of training centers for models and talent, offers a weeklong talent and fashion competition for aspiring models, actors, singers, and dancers, who perform for top fashion and talent agents. Competition categories include Fashion Print, Runway, Commercial Print, Swimwear, Singing, Dancing, Cold Read, Soaps, Sitcom, Theatrical Headshots, Jeans, Toy's R' Us, Monologue, and TV Commercials. Contact the association for more information.

International Modeling and Talent Association
http://www.imta.com

Long Lake Camp for the Arts

Camps

Long Lake Camp for the Arts offers a variety of arts-based programs to young people ages 10 through 16. Programs include Fine Arts, Theatre, Dance, Music, Circus, and Video/Film. The Fine Arts program offers many special studios, which are taught by artists-in-residence. These include Design and Sewing, Drawing, Jewelry, Photography, Silk-Screen Fabric Design, Silversmithing, and Weaving. In addition to program-related activities, campers can participate in sports and outdoor recreational outings. Three- and six-week sessions are available and cost $4,450 and $7,950 respectively. Tuition includes food and lodging, private lessons, craft materials, and all programs of instruction except horseback riding. Contact the Long Lake Camp for the Arts for more information.

Long Lake Camp for the Arts
199 Washington Avenue
Dobbs Ferry, NY 10522-1212
marc@longlakecamp.com
http://www.longlakecamp.com

Oxbow Summer Art Camp

Camps

High school students ages 14 through 16 are eligible to apply for admission to the Oxbow Summer Art Camp, which is located in picturesque Napa Valley, California. The two-and-a-half-week program (which is available in both commuter and residential options) immerses young people in drawing, photography, painting, sculpture, and digital art. Facilities include dormitories, art studios, a dining hall, and an organic garden. Only 36 boarding campers and 26 commuter students are chosen for each session. Tuition for boarding students is approximately $2,800, while commuter students pay about $2,000 (which includes three meals a day). Visit Oxbow's Web site for a virtual tour and more information.

Oxbow Summer Art Camp
530 Third Street
Napa, CA 94559-2702
707-255-6000
summercamp@oxbowschool.org
http://www.oxbowschool.org/summercamp

Pre-College Program at Johns Hopkins University

College Courses/Summer Study

Johns Hopkins University welcomes academically talented high school students to its summertime Pre-College Program. Participants in this program live on Hopkins' Homewood campus for five weeks beginning in early July. They pursue one of more than 20 programs leading to college credit, including Art ("Introductory Photography") and Entrepreneurship and Management ("Introduction to Business"). All participants in the Pre-College Program also attend workshops on college admissions, time management, and diversity. Students who live in the greater Baltimore area have the option of commuting. As of July 1, applicants must be at least 15, have completed their sophomore, junior, or senior year, and have a minimum GPA of 3.0. All applicants must submit an application form, essay, transcript, two recommendations, and a nonrefundable application fee (rates vary by date of submission). For more information about financial aid, costs, deadlines, and to receive an application form, contact the Office of Summer Programs.

Office of Summer Programs/ Pre-College Program
Johns Hopkins University
Wyman Park Building, Suite G4
3400 North Charles Street
Baltimore, MD 21218-2685
800-548-0548
summer@jhu.edu
http://www.jhu.edu/~sumprog/pre-college

Pre-College Programs at the Fashion Institute of Technology (FIT)

College Courses/Summer Study

FIT's Center For Pre-College Programs offers noncredit and credit courses to high school seniors who are interested in fashion. These courses are typically offered during spring and fall semester weekends and during the summer. In addition to taking fashion-related courses, students also take field trips to fashion museums, retailers, industry showrooms, and studios. Vacation Workshops are also available to high school students. Workshops are held in the spring and consist of four sessions totaling 12 hours. Recent Workshops included Beaded Jewelry Design, Caricatures, Creativity 911, Crocheting Summer Fashions, Designer Challenge: Deconstructing and Reconstructing Fashion, Fashion Design and Drawing, Mannequin Madness, and Pattern and Color. Students who complete Vacation Workshops receive a certificate of completion that they can use in their portfolio or submit with their college applications. The cost of each workshop is $95, which includes most supplies. Contact the center for more information.

Pre-College Programs at the Fashion Institute of Technology (FIT)
Seventh Avenue at 27th Street
New York, NY 10001-5992
212-217-7999
FITinfo@fitnyc.edu
http://www.fitnyc.edu/html/dynamic.html

Pre-College Summer Programs at Dickinson College

College Courses/Summer Study

Rising high school juniors and seniors who are interested in exploring careers may want to participate in Pre-College Summer Programs at Dickinson College. The month-long program, available in both residential and commuter options, exposes young people to college-level classes in their field of interest. Recent courses included "Introduction to Photography," "Introduction to Digital Photography," "Marketing," and "Fundamentals of Business." The residential program costs approximately $5,000, which includes accommodations in Dickinson College dormitories, a full meal plan, special events, and field trips. Additional fees for spending money and books are required. Costs for the commuter options were yet to be determined as of press time; contact the director of Summer Programs for further information. Some financial aid is available.

Summer Programs
Dickinson College
Attn: Director of Summer Programs
PO Box 1773
Carlisle, PA 17013-2896
717-254-8782
summer@dickinson.edu
http://www.dickinson.edu/summer/precollege.html

SkillsUSA

Competitions

SkillsUSA offers "local, state and national competitions in which students demonstrate occupational and leadership skills." Students who participate in its SkillsUSA Championships can compete in categories such as Advertising Design, Cosmetology, Customer Service, Nail Care, and Photography. SkillsUSA works directly with high schools and colleges, so ask your guidance counselor or teacher if it is an option for you. Visit the SkillsUSA Web site for more information.

SkillsUSA
PO Box 3000
Leesburg, VA 20177-0300
703-777-8810
http://www.skillsusa.org

Student Photographic Society

Competitions, Membership

College photography students may apply for membership in the society. Membership benefits include job search assistance, a subscription to *Professional Photographer* magazine, a subscription to the *Student Photo Newsletter,* and access to a volunteer program that links members with industry professionals. The society also offers competitions to its members.

Student Photographic Society
229 Peachtree Street, NE, Suite 2200
Atlanta, GA 30303-1608
866-886-5325
info@studentphoto.com
http://www.studentphoto.com

Summer Art Studio at the University of Wisconsin-Green Bay

Camps

Students entering grades 10 through 12 may participate in the University of Wisconsin-Green Bay's Summer Art Studio, a five-day arts immersion camp that is offered with both commuter and residential options. Recent courses included "Metals and Jewelry," "Advanced Photography: Using the Darkroom," and "Street Chic: Creating Your Personal Style in Streetwear." The fee for commuters is $185. The resident fee is $429, which includes instruction, room and board (participants are encouraged to bring a fan because there is no air conditioning in the dorms), supervision by counselors, and evening activity transportation (there is an extra cost for evening activities). Some scholarships are available. The university also offers a Studio Art Program for middle school students. Contact the Office of Outreach and Extension for further information on both programs.

Youth Opportunities Summer Camps
University of Wisconsin-Green Bay
Office of Outreach and Extension
2420 Nicolet Drive
Green Bay, WI 54311-7001
800-892-2118
summercamps@uwgb.edu
http://www.uwgb.edu/camps/html/camps/summerArtHi2006.htm

Summer College for High School Students at Cornell University

College Courses/Summer Study

As part of its Summer College for High School Students, Cornell University offers Exploration seminars for students who have completed their junior or senior years. Explorations are available in Art, Business, College Success, Writing, and other areas. The Summer College session runs for six weeks from late June until early August. It is largely a residential program designed to acquaint you with all aspects of college life. The Exploration seminars allow students to survey various disciplines within the field and speak with working professionals. The seminar meets several times per week and includes lectures and field trips. In addition, Summer College participants take two college-level courses of their own choosing from a total of 60 courses offered. You must bear in mind that these are regular undergraduate courses condensed into a very short time span, so they are especially challenging and demanding. Besides the course material, you will learn time-management and study skills to prepare you for a program of undergraduate study.

Cornell University awards letter grades and full undergraduate credit for the two courses you complete, but none for the Exploration. Residents live and eat on campus, and enjoy access to the university's recreational facilities, the Herbert F. Johnson Museum of Art, and special activities. Academic fees total around $3,400, while housing, food, and recreation fees amount to an additional $1,600. Books, travel, and an application fee are extra. A very limited amount of financial aid is available. Applications are due in early May, although Cornell advises that you submit them well in advance of the deadline; those applying for financial aid must submit their applications by early April. Further information and details of the application procedure are available from the Summer College office.

Summer College for High School Students
Cornell University
B20 Day Hall
Ithaca, NY 14853-2801
607-255-6203
http://www.sce.cornell.edu/sc/explorations/art.php

Summer College for High School Students at Syracuse University

College Courses/Summer Study

The Syracuse University Summer College for High School Students offers a Fashion and Textile Design program for those who have just completed their sophomore, junior, or senior year. The Summer College lasts six weeks and offers a residential option so participants can experience campus life while still in high school. The program has several aims: to introduce you to the many specialties within fashion and textile design; to help you match your aptitudes with possible careers; and to prepare you for college, both academically and socially. It has four modules: Introduction to the World of Fashion, Weaving and Woven Textiles, Introduction to Fashion Knits, and Introduction to Industry Garment Construction. Students work in the studio, listen to lectures, take field trips to fashion and textile sites, and take part in a final exhibition of their work. All students are required to take two courses during the program, and they receive college credit if they successfully complete the courses. Admission is competitive and is based on recommendations, test scores, and transcripts. The total cost of the residential program is about $5,700; the commuter option costs about $4,180. Some scholarships are available. The application deadline is in mid-May, or mid-April for those seeking financial aid. (Note: Programs are also available in Art and Design, Management, Public Communications, and other areas.) For further information, contact the Summer College.

Syracuse University Summer College for High School Students
111 Waverly Avenue, Suite 240
Syracuse, NY 13244-2320
315-443-5297
summcoll@syr.edu
http://summercollege.syr.edu

Summer Program for Secondary School Students at Harvard University

College Courses/Summer Study

High school students who have completed their sophomore, junior, or senior years may apply to Harvard's Summer Program for Secondary School Students. Students who live on campus take either two four-unit courses or one eight-unit course for college credit. Commuting students may take only one four-unit course for college credit. Recent courses included "Introduction to Still Photography," "Feature Writing," and "Principles of Editing." In addition to academics, students can participate in extracurricular activities such as intramural sports, a trivia bowl, a talent show, and dances. Tuition for the program ranges from $2,125 (per four-unit course) to $4,250 (per eight-unit course). A nonrefundable registration fee ($50), health insurance ($110), and room and board ($3,725) are extra. The application deadline for this program is mid-June. Contact the program for more information.

Summer Program for Secondary School Students
Harvard University
51 Brattle Street
Cambridge, MA 02138-3701
617-495-3192
ssp@hudce.harvard.edu
http://www.summer.harvard.edu/2006/programs/ssp.jsp

Summer Programs at Savannah College of Art and Design

College Courses/Summer Study

Students who have completed their junior year of high school can participate in the Rising Star program, a five-week residential program that allows students to experience college-level fashion and design courses. Students who complete the program receive 10 hours of college credit. Rising high school sophomores, juniors, and seniors can participate in Summer Seminars, one-week residential summer workshop programs that focus on fashion- and design-related topics. Students in both programs live in residence halls on campus and receive meals via a college meal plan. Contact the college for information on program costs, dates, and eligibility requirements.

Summer Programs
Savannah College of Art and Design
PO Box 2072
Savannah, GA 31402-2072
800-869-7223
admissions@scad.eedu
http://www.scad.edu/admission/summer_programs/index.cfm

Summer Study at Pennsylvania State University

College Courses/Summer Study

High school students who have completed the 10th, 11th, and 12th grades are eligible to apply for Penn State's Summer Study programs. The six-and-a-half-week College Credit Program begins in late June and offers a variety of classes, including "Introduction to Drawing," "Basic Writing Skills," and "Introduction to Creative Writing." Students typically choose one college credit course (for three or four credits) and either an enrichment class/

workshop or the Kaplan SAT prep class. The three-and-a-half-week Non-Credit Enrichment Program is held in early July and features classes such as "Channel Your Inner Chanel: Fashion and Design," "Say Cheese!: Photography," "For Everything Else, There's: Advertising," "You're Fired!: Business And Marketing," and "Stop the Presses: Journalism/Communications." Students who have completed the 9th, 10th, and 11th grades are eligible for the program. Tuition for the College Credit Program is approximately $6,000, while tuition for the Non-Credit Enrichment Program is approximately $4,000. Limited financial aid is available. Contact the Summer Study Program for more information.

Summer Study Program
900 Walt Whitman Road
Melville, NY 11747-2293
800-666-2556
info@summerstudy.com
http://www.summerstudy.com/pennstate

Texas 4-H Fabric and Fashion Design Competition at the Texas A&M Agricultural Research and Extension Center

Competitions

Texas 4-H members who are high school seniors and who have completed a 4-H clothing project with an emphasis on fabric and fashion design may enter the Texas 4-H Fabric and Fashion Design Competition. There are three competition categories: Accessory Design, Apparel Design, and Textile Design. Within each category, competitors must choose between original design and pattern modification. Applicants must submit a portfolio and participate in an interview. A panel of judges will choose winners for each category. Contact the Texas A&M Agricultural Research and Extension Center for more information.

Texas 4-H Fabric and Fashion Design Competition
Texas A&M Agricultural Research and Extension Center
2251 TAMU
College Station, TX 77843-2251
http://fcs.tamu.edu/clothing/4h/packet/design_competition.php

Read a Book

When it comes to finding out about fashion careers, don't overlook a book. (You're reading one now, after all.) What follows is a short, annotated list of books and periodicals related to fashion. The books range from personal accounts of what it's like to be a fashion designer to professional volumes on specific topics, such as photography techniques, to advice on breaking into the fashion industry. Don't be afraid to check out the professional journals, either. The technical stuff may be way above your head right now, but if you take the time to become familiar with one or two, you're bound to pick up some of what is important to fashion professionals, not to mention begin to feel like a part of their world, which is what you're interested in, right?

We've tried to include recent materials as well as old favorites. Always check for the most recent editions, and, if you find an author you like, ask your librarian to help you find more. Keep reading good books and magazines!

❑ BOOKS

Agins, Teri. *The End of Fashion: How Marketing Changed the Clothing Business Forever.* New York: Harper Paperbacks, 2000. This book explores the fundamental changes in the fashion industry—from manufacturing, retailing, licensing, image making, and financing—since the stock market crash of October 19, 1987.

All About Techniques in Illustration. Hauppauge, N.Y.: Barron's Educational Series, 2001. Using black-and-white and color media, this book shows students how to professionally complete illustrations for advertising, books, and more.

Amphlett, Hilda. *Hats: A History of Fashion in Headwear.* Mineola, N.Y.: Dover Publications, 2003. This comprehensive book, with more than 800 illustrations, documents chronologically, by century, more than 2,000 years of head coverings—a subject that encompasses many eras and nationalities.

Armstrong, Helen Joseph. *Patternmaking for Fashion Design.* 4th ed. Upper Saddle River, N.J.: Prentice Hall, 2005. Known for its comprehensive coverage, exceptional illustrations, and clear instructions, this hallmark book offers detailed yet easy-to-understand explanations of the essence of patternmaking.

Breward, Christopher. *Fashion.* New York: Oxford University Press, 2003. From haute couture, High Street, and developing fabric technology, to such fashion industry stars as Coco Chanel, Giorgio Armani, and Alexander McQueen, this book explores aspects of the fashion industry far beyond style and function. Following 150 years of fashion, it offers a colorful and flamboyant description of the industry's trends, products, and inhabitants.

Brunson-Sarrabo, Yolanda. *The Ins and Outs of the Fashion Industry—From a Fashion Insider.* Lincoln, Nebr.: iUniverse, Inc., 2005. For individuals interested in finding a job in the world of fashion, this book offers guidelines, advice, and secrets on how to achieve success in this competitive business. Topics covered include interviewing techniques, necessary education and skills, and the pros and cons of working in the industry.

Burns, Leslie Davis, and Nancy O. Bryant. *The Business of Fashion: Designing, Manufacturing, and Marketing.* 2d ed. New York: Fairchild Books & Visuals, 2002. This useful reference book, covering all aspects of the fashion industry, provides charts, important contacts, and calendars of events that will be of interest to anyone starting a fashion business or wanting to find a job in fashion. Also included are valuable explanations of career opportunities and jobs in the industry.

Buxbaum, Gerda (ed.). *Icons Of Fashion: The 20th Century.* New York: Prestel Publishing, 2005. This best-selling book provides an overview of the 20th-century fashion world through a comprehensive collection of photographs, drawings, and fascinating historical text.

Cox, Mary. *2005 Artist's & Graphic Designer's Market.* Cincinnati, Ohio: Writers Digest Books, 2004. Important resource published annually for artists and designers, with more than 2,300 industry contacts. Contact information includes submission requirements, payment policies, Web sites, and other guidelines. Also includes valuable articles and tips from industry pros.

Derrick, Robin, and Robin Muir. *Unseen Vogue: The Secret History of Fashion Photography.* New York: Little Brown and Company, 2004. A visual catalog of fashion, this book serves as a tribute to the artists, photographers, and beauties featured in *Vogue* magazine over the course of many decades.

Dickerson, Kitty G., and Jeannette Jarnow. *Inside the Fashion Business.* 7th ed. Upper Saddle River, N.J.: Prentice Hall, 2002. Written by authors with extensive industry ties and business savvy, the text provides an overview of the fashion sectors from a business perspective.

Edwards, Betty. *New Drawing on the Right Side of the Brain Workbook: Guided Practice in the Five Basic Skills of Drawing.* New York: Jeremy P. Tarcher, 2002. Forty exercises are presented that cover the five basic skills of drawing. This book focuses largely on portraits done in pencil, but also touches on other subject matter and mediums.

Fleishman, Michael. *Starting Your Career as a Freelance Illustrator or Graphic Designer.* New York: Watson-Guptill Publications, 2001. Shows readers how to analyze which markets are right for their work and land those jobs, and details how to prepare a winning portfolio, make contacts, price one's work, order supplies and equipment, and more. Also covers important Internet tools for illustrators and graphic designers.

Frankel, Susannah. *Visionaries: Interviews With Fashion Designers.* London, U.K.: Victoria & Albert Publications, 2001. This book, a collection of the author's previously published interviews with fashion designers, offers a penetrating look into some of the world's most intriguing design professionals.

Frost, Lee. *The A–Z of Creative Photography: Over 70 Techniques Explained in Full.* New York: Watson-Guptill Publications, 1998. Provides techniques and tips to better photography, with color and black-and-white photos to illustrate each suggestion.

Gallanis, Peter J., and Jennifer James. *FabJob Guide to Become a Fashion Designer.* Seattle, Wash.: FabJob Inc., 2005. This book for beginners teaches you how to get started and succeed as a fashion designer. It serves as a useful guidebook for anyone who wants to break into the business, no matter what his or her experience level.

Grealy, Lucy. *Autobiography of a Face.* New York: Harper Perennial, 2003. Diagnosed with Ewing's sarcoma at the age of nine, the author details her life as a disfigured child and young adult. This important book about image—and one person's endless quest for beauty—details what it means to feel both ugly and special at the same time. (See also *Truth & Beauty: A Friendship,* by Ann Patchett.)

Grimm, Tom, and Michele Grimm. *Basic Book of Photography.* 5th ed. New York: Plume Books, 2003. Respected handbook for both beginning and experienced photographers. Includes close to 400 instructive illustrations and a glossary, as well as a new chapter on digital cameras and imaging.

Gross, Elaine, and Fred Rottman. *Halston: An American Original.* New York: HarperCollins, 1999. This comprehensive survey of Halston's work is based on exclusive interviews with the people who knew and worked with Halston throughout his turbulent career. Interviews with celebrities as well as contemporary designers are highlighted.

Hagen, Kathryn. *Illustration For Designers.* 2d ed. Portland, Oreg.: Hagen Publishing, 2000. This fashion-drawing textbook contains more than 600 illustrations of various poses and garments, step-by-step drawing charts, and proportion templates for flats, fashion heads, and male and female figures.

Han, Holly. *Vault Career Guide to the Fashion Industry.* New York: Vault, Inc., 2003. This book breaks down the functions of different careers in fashion. Detailed looks at typical days for buyers, designers, and interior designers are included.

Jones, Sue Jenkyn. *Fashion Design.* 2d ed. New York: Watson-Guptill Publications, 2005. This definitive reference offers an authoritative, balanced overview of the fashion business today for anyone who is considering a career in the industry. It describes the qualities and skills needed to become a fashion designer and examines the wide range of additional career opportunities available.

Kellogg, Ann T., Amy T. Peterson, et al. *In an Influential Fashion: An Encyclopedia of Nineteenth- and Twentieth-Century Fashion Designers and Retailers Who Transformed Dress.* Westport, Conn.: Greenwood Press, 2002. The text closely examines the relationship between cultural development and style. Entries were chosen because their influence on fashion is reflective of societal, political, or economic change—not for their artistic merit alone.

Koda, Harold. *Extreme Beauty: The Body Transformed.* New York: Metropolitan Museum of Art, 2004. Weaving anthropology, sociology, art history, and haute couture into a survey of shifting notions of the beautiful body, this book surveys fashion's literal imprint on the body, while tracing the history of clothing styles.

London, Barbara, John Upton, Kenneth Kobre, and Betsy Brill. *Photography.* 8th ed. Upper Saddle River, N.J.: Prentice Hall, 2001. Teaches beginners how to use techniques and visual awareness to hone their craft. Also includes detailed instruction on digital imaging and other technological advances.

Matheson, Eve. *The Modeling Handbook.* 4th ed. Boca Raton, Fla.: Peter Glenn Publications, 2000. Written by a freelance writer and mother of a former professional model, this handbook offers practical advice to models and their parents.

Mauro, Lucia, Kathy Siebel, and Maureen Costello. *Careers for Fashion Plates & Other Trendsetters.* 2d ed. New York: McGraw-Hill/Contemporary Books, 2002. Part of the Careers for You series, meant to inspire career explorers to look at the job market through the lens of their own interests, this book discusses how to turn your passion for fashion into a successful, profitable career.

McGrath, Jinks. *Basic Jewelry Making Techniques.* London, U.K.: Chartwell Books, 2003. This book shows how, after mastering only a few basic techniques, crafting even the most complicated jewelry pieces becomes an easy task. Readers will learn to use techniques such as soldering, texturing, and enameling on wood, acrylic, glass, precious stones, and more.

McKinney, Anne (ed.). *Real-Resumes for Retailing, Modeling, Fashion and Beauty Industry Jobs: Including Real Resumes Used to Change Careers and Transfer Skills to Other Industries.* Fayetteville, N.C.: Prep Publishing, 2002. Jobs in retailing, modeling, and the fashion business can be difficult to obtain. This book provides the competitive edge, offering advice for those who are just starting their search and for those who are making career changes.

Model & Talent Directory: International Directory of Model and Talent Agencies and Schools. Boca Raton, Fla.: Peter Glenn Publications, 2004. This directory is updated and published annually.

Moellers, Marcia Rothschild. *So, You Want to Be a Fashion Model?* New York: Interscout, LLC, 2003. Written for young teenagers and their parents, this book outlines the nuts and bolts of getting a child into modeling.

National Association of Schools of Art and Design Directory 2004. Reston, Va.: National Association of Schools of Art and Design. Annual publication that lists accredited art institutions and degree programs.

Newman, Cathy. *Fashion.* Washington, D.C.: National Geographic Society, 2003. Providing a fascinating global perspective on the historical and cultural significance of clothing and adornment, this timeless subject is explored in evocative essays and lavish illustrations that offer a fresh perspective for today's style-obsessed culture.

Olver, Elizabeth. *The Art of Jewelry Design: From Idea to Reality.* Cincinnati, Ohio: North Light Books, 2002. This visually stunning guide provides readers with the techniques and advice they need to transform jewelry designs into reality.

Paleczny, Barbara. *Clothed in Integrity: Weaving Just Cultural Relations and the Garment Industry.* Waterloo, Ont.: Wilfrid Laurier University Press, 2000. Assessing the responsibility of transnational retailers for unacceptable wages and working conditions, this book describes historic shifts in the global context of garment production. It also sets out short-term and long-term actions for changing the situation.

Patchett, Ann. *Truth & Beauty: A Friendship.* New York: Perennial, 2005. This memoir—a celebration of friendship between the author of *Autobiography of a Face* (see the separate entry for this book written by Lucy Grealy) and Ann Patchett—begins in college when they met and continues through middle life. Told through bursts of dialogue and memories, this is the story of a relationship between two women—one who has medical and emotional problems that deteriorate into drug addiction and thoughts of suicide—that is refreshingly honest.

Posen, Zac. *The Fashion Designer Survival Guide: An Insider's Look at Starting and Running Your Own Fashion Business.* Chicago: Dearborn Trade Publishing, 2005. Offering readers behind-the-scenes advice and essential business information on creating and sustaining a successful career as an independent designer, this book provides case studies from independent designers at different stages in their careers—from tough let-downs to exciting successes.

Press, Debbie. *Your Modeling Career.* New York: Allworth Press, 2004. Covering the latest technology and the impact of reality TV on the modeling industry, this comprehensive guide reveals how to be a successful model without being a superstar or drop-dead gorgeous.

Rose, Yvonne, and Tony Rose. *Is Modeling for You?: The Handbook and Guide for the Young Aspiring Black Model.* Phoenix, Ariz.: Amber Books, 1998.

This first and only comprehensive book on modeling written for and about the African-American model is a useful guidebook and resource for African Americans trying to break into the modeling business.

Sammon, Rick. *Rick Sammon's Complete Guide to Digital Photography: 107 Lessons on Taking, Making, Editing, Storing, Printing, and Sharing Better Digital Images.* New York: W. W. Norton & Company, 2003. Digital photography advice from one of North America's most widely read photo columnists. More than 1,000 images that detail shooting and Photoshop techniques.

Samuel, Wendy. *Fashion Careers: The Complete Job Search Workbook.* 3d ed. New York: Fashion Careers, 2003. This definitive guide for anyone looking for a job in fashion or fashion-related industries includes an up-to-date list of job-search Web sites, a new research section including URLs for fashion industry publications and organizations, and a brand new section on Internet job search techniques.

Schaub, George. *Using Your Camera, A Basic Guide to 35mm Photography.* Revised ed. New York: Amphoto Books, 2002. Excellent beginner's guide, covering topics such as camera functions, composition, and different light exposures.

Seeling, Charlotte. *Fashion: The Century of the Designer, 1900-1999.* Osceola, Wisc.: Konemann, 2000. This book provides information, decade by decade, about influential designers of the century.

Stephens Frings, Gini. *Fashion: From Concept to Consumer.* 8th ed. Upper Saddle River, N.J.: Prentice Hall, 2004. This textbook tells the story of how the fashion business works, in sequential order, from concept to consumer. It provides an overview of the design, manufacturing, and retail sectors of the fashion industry.

Summers, Barbara. *Black and Beautiful: How Women of Color Changed the Fashion Industry.* New York: Amistad Press, 2001. This book highlights more than 60 years of triumphs and struggles for black women in the fashion modeling business.

Tain, Linda. *Portfolio Presentation for Fashion Designers.* 2d ed. New York: Fairchild Publications, 2003. This comprehensive guide to creating a fashion portfolio shows you how to create a dynamic, professional portfolio. With more than 300 illustrations ranging from sketches by newcomers to the work of top designers, this book offers hundreds of concrete tips.

Tarantino, Chris, and Kevin Tan. *Digital Fashion Photography.* Boston: Course Technology, 2005. Geared toward both professionals and people working to become professionals, this book offers essential instruction on digital fashion photography.

Varley, Rosemary. *Retail Product Management: Buying and Merchandising.* 2d ed. New York: Routledge, 2005. Covering all retail operations—from those that revolve around the procurement of products, to stock level management, through allocation of outlet space for products, to the placement of products within the retail environment—this book is essential reading for anyone studying retail product management of buying and merchandising.

Watson, Linda. *20th Century Fashion.* Richmond Hill, Ont.: Firefly Books Ltd., 2004. This book, in association with *Vogue* magazine, chronicles more than a century of fashion, celebrating the most significant designers, developments, and movements of each decade.

Wilcox, Claire. *Radical Fashion.* London, U.K.: Victoria & Albert Museum, 2001. The official publication of the exhibition of the same name at the Victoria and Albert Museum, London, Radical Fashion spotlights the work of 11 designers. Stunning photo-essays, paired with stimulating commentary by curators and fashion historians, make this book the ultimate accessory for anyone addicted to style.

❑ PERIODICALS

The Apparel Strategist. Published monthly for the apparel and textile industries, this resource offers retail sales and performance figures, consumer data, and financial performance profiles. To subscribe, contact PO Box 406, Fleetwood, PA 19522-0406, 866-944-5995, subscribe@apparelstrategist.com, http://www.apparelstrategist.com.

California Apparel News. Published weekly by CaliforniaMart (110 East Ninth Street, Suite A-777, Los Angeles, CA 90079-1777, 213-627-3737, http://www.apparelnews.net) on Fridays since 1945, this newspaper reports and analyzes the latest trends in the apparel industry. Buyers, manufacturers, suppliers, trade show organizations, and educational institutions alike utilize it.

Cosmopolitan. Published monthly by Hearst Communications, Inc. (PO Box 7162, Red Oak, IA 51591-0162), this magazine offers the latest in fashion, beauty, health, relationship, and celebrity news. It is the best-selling young women's monthly magazine in the world. Visit http://www.cosmopolitan.com to read sample articles.

CosmoGIRL! Published monthly by Hearst Communications, Inc. (PO Box 7791, Red Oak, IA 51591-0791), this magazine is the teen-friendly version of Cosmopolitan, covering topics of interest to teen girls—guys, beauty and fashion, entertainment, and female empowerment. Visit http://www.cosmogirl.com to read sample articles.

Daily News Record. Published by Fairchild Publications, Inc., PO Box 15428, North Hollywood, CA 91615-5428, 800-360-1700, custserv@espcomp.com, http://www.dnrnews.com. With a readership comprised of fashion industry insiders—from buyers and merchandisers to designers and textile executives— *DNR* has become a leader in the men's fashion and retail industry.

Dress: The Journal of The Costume Society of America. Published annually by the Costume Society of America, 203 Towne Centre Drive, Hillsborough, NJ, 08844-4693, 800-CSA-9447, national.office@costumesocietyamerica.com, http://www.costumesocietyamerica.com/dress.htm. The journal aims to place costume in a cultural and historical context by offering articles, book and exhibition reviews, letters to the editor, and short reports to its membership.

Elle. Published monthly by Hachette Filipacchi Media, U.S., Inc., elle@neodata.com, https://www.neodata.com/hfmus/elle/print_subs.shtml. This magazine prides itself on providing a sophisticated look at the latest in fashion, beauty, and style. Visit http://www.elle.com to read sample articles.

ELLEgirl. Published monthly by Hachette Filipacchi Media, U.S., Inc., http://www.hfmus.com/HachetteUSA/Page.asp?Site=ElleGirl. This magazine, available by print and digital subscription, targets fashion-forward, global-thinking, independent, and sophisticated young women. Visit http://www.ellegirl.com to read sample articles.

Esquire. Published monthly by Hearst Communications, Inc., PO Box 7529, Red Oak, IA 51591-0529, 800-925-0485. This is a fashion, health, money, and celebrity news magazine aimed at lending a fresh, sophisticated perspective to men's issues. Visit http://www.esquire.com to read sample articles.

Fashion Theory: The Journal of Dress, Body and Culture. Published quarterly by Berg Publishers, Angel Court, 81 St. Clements Street, Oxford OX4 1AW United Kingdom, http://www.bergpublishers.com. *Fashion Theory* offers a critical analysis of dress, from clothing to body art. Looking at dress as a cultural construction makes *Fashion Theory* useful reading for fashion, art, cultural studies, and anthropology students alike.

Footwear News. Published weekly by Fairchild Publications, Inc., PO Box 15877, North Hollywood, CA 91615-5877, 800-360-1700, fn@espcomp.com, http://www.footwearnews.com. For 60 years, *Footwear News* has provided footwear industry insiders the latest in men's, women's, and children's footwear trends in broad-ranging categories, from casual to workboots.

Glamour. Published monthly by Condé Nast, 4 Times Square, 17th Floor, New York, NY 10036-6518, 800-274-7410, *Glamour* is a fashion, beauty, celebrity, relationship, and lifestyle women's monthly magazine offering features, advice columns, and contests. Visit http://www.glamour.com to read sample articles.

GQ. Published monthly by Condé Nast, 4 Times Square, 17th Floor, New York, NY 10036-6518, 800-289-9330. This men's fashion and culture magazine features articles on fashion as well as on politics, entertainment, and sports. *GQ* aims to identify new male trends and trendsetters. Visit http://men.style.com/gq to read sample articles.

Harper's Bazaar. Published monthly by Hearst Communications, Inc., PO Box 7162, Red Oak, IA 51591-0529. This women's monthly fashion, beauty, and celebrity magazine offers fashion advice and the latest in fashion news. Visit http://www.harpersbazaar.com to read sample articles.

Hint. This online magazine offers a variety of features and columns for those interested in the retail, fashion, modeling, and fashion photography industries. Visit http://www.hintmag.com to read sample articles.

InStyle. Published 13 times annually by Time Inc., 1271 Avenue of the Americas, 26th Floor, New York, NY 10020, 800-274-6200. Readers looking for a mix of fashion, beauty, celebrity, and lifestyle news will find *In Style* on top of the latest trends. Just over 10 years old, this fashion/lifestyle magazine has quickly become a favorite amongst readers interested in celebrity fashion. Visit http://www.instyle.com to read sample articles.

NEA ARTS. Bimonthly newsletter published by the National Endowment for the Arts (NEA). Covers the NEA's national initiatives and programs, awards, and grants. Also includes a calendar of NEA events, available online (http://www.arts.gov/about/NEARTS/index.html) only in Portable Document Format (PDF).

Professional Photographer. Published monthly by the Professional Photographers of America, 229 Peachtree Street, NE, Suite 2200, International Tower, Atlanta, GA 30303-1601, 800-742-7468, ppa@bframe.com, http://www.ppa.com. Offers useful information for aspiring and practicing photographers. Includes business and artistic tips, equipment and technology profiles, interviews with well-known photographers, and industry information.

Style. Published monthly by Style Communications, Inc., 555 Richmond Street West, Suite 701, Toronto, ON M5V 3B1 Canada, 416-203-6737, style@style.ca. *Style* is a Canadian-based fashion magazine that serves as a source for apparel trends, merchandising solutions, fashion technology, and runway news. Its readership is women's and men's wear designers, retailers, and students. Visit http://www.style.ca/index.jsp to read sample articles.

Vogue. Published monthly by Condé Nast, 4 Times Square, 17th Floor, New York, NY 10036-6518, 800-234-2347, talkingback@vogue.com. Though *Vogue* is often thought of as the industry standard fashion magazine, it is also known to include current events and celebrity news features, as well. Visit http://www.style.com/vogue to read sample articles.

Voice: AIGA Journal of Design. American Institute of Graphic Arts. Online journal of the American Institute of Graphic Arts. Offers useful articles about trends and issues in graphic design. Also offers an online forum that readers can use to share their ideas or feedback regarding articles. You can read the publication by visiting http://journal.aiga.org.

W. Published monthly by Condé Nast, 4 Times Square, 17th Floor, New York, NY 10036-6518, 800-289-0390. This women's fashion magazine is geared specifically toward high-end, haute couture fashionistas. Monthly articles feature the latest from the runway, design tables, and high society events.

Visit http://www.style.com/w to read sample articles.

Women's Wear Daily. Published by Fairchild Publications, Inc., PO Box 15428, North Hollywood, CA 91615-5428, 800-289-0273, custservice@wwd.com. This "fashion bible" offers readers business news and insight into trends in the fashion, beauty, and retail industries. Readership is comprised of industry insiders, socialites, and trendsetters. Visit http://www.wwd.com to read sample articles.

Surf the Web

You must use the Internet to do research and to explore. The Internet is the closest you'll get to what's happening right now all around the world. This chapter gets you started with an annotated list of Web sites related to fashion. Try a few. Follow the links. Maybe even venture as far as asking questions in a chat room. The more you read about and interact with fashion personnel, the better prepared you'll be when you're old enough to participate as a professional.

One caveat: you probably already know that URLs change all the time. If a Web address listed below is out of date, try searching on the site's name or other key words. Chances are if it's still out there, you'll find it. If it's not, maybe you'll find something better!

About.Com: Style/ Women's Fashion

http://fashion.about.com

With articles written by Cynthia Nellis, a fashion journalist and former fashion buyer, this Web site contains up-to-date information on all the latest fashion trends and styles. If you want to catch up on the hottest boots or handbag styles, this Web site has this and so much more—from celebrity style to information on fashion careers and education. If you're thinking about a career in fashion, be sure to check out a series of articles called, "A Day in the Life of a Fashion Professional."

Beauty Matters.com

http://www.beautymatters.blogspot.com

This Web site offers an exploration into the nature of beauty. With minimal graphics, its primary goal is to discuss beauty and where our ideas of beauty come from. Intelligently written by Lindie Pavati, Ph.D., an Italian teacher, artist, and musician, this site is designed to be read by anyone seeking original, quality information on the culture of beauty. Students and teachers interested in research on a variety of beauty-related topics can also find information and advice on how to incorporate ideas into classroom teaching.

Career Threads.com

http://www.careerthreads.com

Almost everybody in the world wears clothes. That means there are plenty of career opportunities for anyone interested in producing garments for a living. This Web site provides an introduction into the many careers available in this exciting industry. With sections providing real-world advice and advice from the pros, this Web site offers practical and informative material on how to get started in a fashion career. You'll also find potential job openings and paid internship opportunities! A very useful Web site.

E-MODEL.NET

http://www.e-model.net

For the wannabe model, this Web site contains a wealth of advice on the business. Familiar with breakdown service, book outs, residuals, and scale wages? If not, these are just a few of the professional modeling terms defined on the site. Sample model contracts, vouchers, and model releases are also provided. Aspiring models should also learn how to protect themselves by reading the section on modeling scams.

Fashion Club

http://www.fashionclub.com

Created by the Fashion Institute of Design & Merchandising, this Web site for teens who are passionate about design—whether it is fashion, interiors, graphics, or visual arts—offers up-to-date fashion and entertainment news. It also provides educational information in its Career Studio, with links to campus tours of the institute's four California campuses.

Fashion Net: How to Become a Fashion Photographer

http://www.fashion.net/howto/photography

Interested in a career in fashion photography? It doesn't have to be an impossible dream, according to three industry insiders who offer tips for getting started. With resources for beginning photographers, including workshops and galleries, tips on darkroom technique, and processing advice, this Web site informs and inspires those who are in the beginning stages of learning about the industry. If you're interested in knowing what your peers think about your work, you can post your own photos to be critiqued

Fashion Planet

http://www.fashion-planet.com

Offering an international view of the world of luxury fashion, this comprehensive Web site covers the fashion industry's finest collections, trends, personalities, and lifestyles from around the world. With features on goings-on in cities such as Rome, New York, and Bangkok, Fashion Planet offers an online monthly magazine that showcases the largest collection of luxury brands on the Internet. Combining the worlds of fashion and technology, the Web site also offers a virtual window-shopping tour of New York.

Fashion Worlds

http://fashionworlds.blogspot.com

With backgrounds in fashion, design, art history, graphics, and computing, the students who contribute to this Web site, who are from villages across Dorset in the United Kingdom, provide up-to-date information on hot designers and trends in the fashion world. You'll find original articles and news updates as well as detailed information about the influences of past and present fashion designers. This Web site is a "must visit" for serious students interested in fashion design.

FashionBook.com
http://www.fashionbook.com

This fascinating Web site of online portfolios, products, and services showcases the industry's top talent. Featuring portfolios of makeup artists, hair stylists, body painters, fashion stylists, photographers, and more, this Web site offers a visual exploration of what working professionals in the business of fashion and beauty are creating today.

FASHION-ERA
http://www.fashion-era.com

This content-rich Web site contains detailed information and illustrations of everything from current fashion trends to the history of fashion from 1750 to present. Highlighting not only fashion and costume history but also social history, this Web site analyzes the influences of technology, culture, and politics on the clothing of an era. A fashion-era forum also provides the opportunity to post questions to message boards covering any number of fashion-related topics.

Fashion-Schools.org
http://www.fashion-schools.org

If you think you want to work in fashion, this Web site will educate you about career options and the training needed for each of them. Whether you think you want to own your own boutique, create accessories, or write fashion articles, this Web site profiles a wide variety of fashion careers. It's also a great resource for those who might be unsure about which direction they want to pursue. Students who are researching their career options can learn about specific fashion schools—the programs and training they provide—and request information about their programs.

Infomat.com
http://www.infomat.com

This fashion industry information services and search engine provides access to more than 350,000 international designers, showrooms, retailers, manufacturers, and suppliers of apparel, textiles, and accessories. Infomat's database is compiled from public sources and is an excellent Web site to search for up-to-date facts and figures about the industry. Discover articles about low-rise jeans in Japan, fashion design from concept to consumer, or global exporting. This Web site serves primarily as a starting point for researching any topic related to the fashion industry.

Modeling Advice
http://www.modelingadvice.com

This small-scale Web site offers very basic advice for young women interested in learning more about the modeling industry. It serves as a starting point by detailing types of modeling, how to find work, and how to behave on a photo shoot. The links provided for major modeling agencies in New York are a valuable resource.

Modeling Scams
http://www.modelingscams.org

Extensive research has shown the common denominator in almost all modeling scams is upfront fees. In other words, you'll never be asked to pay anything upfront by any reputable agency! Most Web sites discussing the business of the modeling industry list some kind of disclaimer about scams. This Web site, devoted in its entirety to helping the aspiring model avoid every scam known to exist, is a must-read for anyone just starting out in modeling. Though most of the information provided is a matter of common sense, the presence of such a Web site proves that it is young, hopeful models who get taken advantage of by not being educated about the common business practices of the industry.

Models.com
http://models.com

This glossy Web site has the look and feel of a commercial, high-fashion magazine. For the latest modeling industry news, and lists of the top 50 female and male fashion models (and photos of course), check out this flashy Web site. For a $59.95 one-year membership, wannabe models can build their own online portfolios, gain access to online chats and interviews with real models, and "get seen" by agents.

My Fashion Life
http://www.myfashionlife.com

This Web site claims to be "for those with a passion for fashion and other things..." With banner ads for Web sites like makepovertyhistory.org, this Web site offers articles, interviews, and news on designers, celebrities, and models, along with a dose of social consciousness. Of particular interest to those who are serious about the fashion industry is the events diary, with links to fashion events, workshops, and seminars on a variety of fashion industry topics (primarily in New York and London).

The New York Times: Fashion & Style
http://www.nytimes.com/pages/fashion

This Web site is a must-bookmark page for anyone who is serious about starting a career in the fashion industry. Daily reading of the style-centered goings-on in New York and the world is essential for successful fashion industry businesspeople. This page contains daily articles on trends, styles, and fashion events in New York—the center of the fashion industry in the United States. You'll also find reviews of runway shows from around the world, important news, and entertaining editorials.

Style.com
http://www.style.com

The online home to *Vogue* and *W* magazines, this Web site is full of photos and articles on fashion shows, fashion industry news and trends, beauty, and people and parties. Unique to the Web site edition—online shopping. If you see something you like, you can order it immediately. Another benefit for true fashion industry buffs is the online newsletter sign-up. Get daily and weekly Style News, Fashion Flash, and Shop News delivered to your inbox for free.

Ask for Money

By the time most students get around to thinking about applying for scholarships, grants, and other financial aid, they have already extolled their personal, academic, and artistic virtues to such lengths in essays, interviews, and portfolios for college applications that even their own grandmothers wouldn't recognize them. The thought of filling out yet another application form fills students with dread. And why bother? Won't the same five or six kids who have been competing for academic and artistic honors for years walk away with all the really good scholarships?

The truth is, most of the scholarships available to high school and college students are being offered because an organization wants to promote interest in a particular field, encourage more students to become qualified to enter it, and finally, to help those students afford an education. Certainly, having a great portfolio or good grade point average is a valuable asset. More often than not, however, grade point averages aren't even mentioned; the focus is on the area of interest and what a student has done to distinguish himself or herself in that area. In fact, sometimes the only requirement is that the scholarship applicant must be studying in a particular area.

❑ GUIDELINES

When applying for scholarships, there are a few simple guidelines that can help ease the process considerably.

Plan Ahead

The absolute worst thing you can do is wait until the last minute. Keep in mind that obtaining recommendations or other supporting data in time to meet an application deadline is incredibly difficult. And no one does his or her best thinking or writing under pressure. So get off to a good start by reviewing scholarship applications as early as possible—months, even a year, in advance. If the current scholarship information isn't available, ask for a copy of last year's version. Once you have the scholarship information or application in hand, give it a thorough read. Try to determine how your experience or situation best fits into the scholarship, or if it even fits at all. Don't waste your time applying for a scholarship in literature if you couldn't finish *Great Expectations.*

If possible, research the award or scholarship, including past recipients and, where applicable, the person in whose name the scholarship is offered. Often, scholarships are established to memorialize an individual who was well known in the fashion industry. In this instance, try to get a feel for the spirit of the person's work. If you have any similar interests, experiences, or abilities, don't hesitate to mention them.

Talk to others who received the scholarship, or to students currently studying in the same area or field of interest in which the scholarship is offered, and try to gain insight into possible applications or work related to that field. When you're working on the essay asking why you want this scholarship, you'll have real answers.

Take your time writing the essays. Make sure you are answering the question or questions on the application and not merely restating facts about yourself. Don't be afraid to get creative; try to imagine what you would think of if you had to sift through hundreds of applications. What would you want to know about the candidate? What would convince you that someone was deserving of the scholarship? Work through several drafts and have someone whose advice you respect—a parent, teacher, or guidance counselor—review the essay for grammar and content.

Finally, if you know in advance which scholarships you want to apply for, there might still be time to stack the deck in your favor by getting an internship, volunteering, or working part time. Bottom line: the more you know about a scholarship and the sooner you learn it, the better.

Follow Directions

Think of it this way: many of the organizations that offer scholarships devote 99.9 percent of their time to something other than the scholarship for which you are applying. Don't make a nuisance of yourself by pestering them for information. Simply follow the directions as they are presented to you. If the scholarship application specifies that you write for further information, then write for it—don't call.

Pay close attention to whether you're applying for an award, a scholarship, a prize, or financial aid. Often these words are used interchangeably, but just as often they have different meanings. An award is usually given for something you have done: built a park or helped distribute meals to the elderly; or something you have created: a work of art, a design, an essay, a short film, a screenplay, or an invention. On the other hand, a scholarship is frequently a renewable sum of money that is given to a person to help defray the costs of college. Scholarships are given to candidates who meet the necessary criteria based on artistic ability, essays, eligibility, grades, or sometimes all four.

Supply all the necessary documents, information, and fees, and make the deadlines. You won't win any scholarships by forgetting to include a recommendation from a teacher or failing to postmark the application by the deadline. Get it right the first time, and get it done on time.

Apply Early

Once you have the application in hand, don't dawdle. If you've requested it far enough in advance, there shouldn't be any reason for you not to turn it in well in advance of the deadline. You never know, if it comes down to two candidates, your timeliness just might be the deciding factor!

Be Yourself

Don't make promises you can't keep. There are plenty of hefty scholarships available, but if they all require you to study something that you don't enjoy, you'll be miserable in college. And the side effects from switching majors after you've accepted a scholarship could be even worse. Be yourself.

Don't Limit Yourself

There are many sources for scholarships, beginning with your guidance counselor and ending with the Internet. All of the search engines have education categories. Start there and search by keywords, such as "financial aid," "scholarship," and "award." And go beyond the scholarships listed on these pages.

If you know of an organization related to or involved with the field of your choice, write a letter asking if they offer scholarships. If they don't offer scholarships, don't stop there. Write them another letter, or better yet, schedule a meeting with the president or someone in the public relations office and ask if they would be willing to sponsor a scholarship for you. Of course, you'll need to prepare yourself well for such a meeting because you're selling a priceless commodity—yourself. Be confident. Tell them all about yourself, what you want to study and why, and let them know what you would be willing to do in exchange—volunteer at their favorite charity, write up reports on your progress in school, or work part time on school breaks, full time during the summer. Explain why you're a wise investment. The sky's the limit!

❑ THE LIST

American Legion Auxiliary
777 North Meridian Street,
Third Floor
Indianapolis, IN 46204-1420
317-955-3845
alahq@legion-aux.org
http://www.legion-aux.org/scholarships/index.aspx

Various state auxiliaries of the American Legion, as well as its national organization, offer scholarships to help students prepare for various careers. Most require that candidates be associated with the organization in some way, whether as a child, spouse, etc., of a military veteran. Interested students should contact the auxiliary for further information.

Art Institute of Seattle
2323 Elliott Avenue
Seattle, WA 98121-1642
800-275-2471
http://www.ais.edu/financial.asp

The Art Institute of Seattle offers associate of applied arts degrees in fashion design, fashion marketing, and photography. It also offers an associate of applied arts and a bachelor of fine arts in graphic design. The Institute provides a wide variety of financial aid to students. Visit its Web site for more information. (Note: There are 31 Art Institutes located throughout the United States and Canada. Visit http://www.aii.edu for a complete list.)

Association on American Indian Affairs
Scholarship Coordinator
966 Hungerford Drive, Suite 12-B
Rockville, MD 20850-1714
240-314-7155
general.aaia@verizon.net
http://www.indian-affairs.org

Native American undergraduate and graduate students who are pursuing a variety of college majors (including fashion) can apply for several different scholarships ranging from $500 to $1,500. All applicants must provide proof of Native American heritage. Visit the Association's Web site for more information.

Berkeley College
Central Admissions Office
Box 440
Little Falls, NJ 07424-0440
financialaid@BerkeleyCollege.edu
http://www.berkeleycollege.edu/Finances/Index.htm

Berkeley College offers associate and bachelor's degrees in fashion marketing and management at its six campuses in New Jersey and New York. More than 20 scholarships and grants are available to students who attend the college. Visit its Web site for more information.

California Alliance for Arts Education
495 East Colorado Boulevard
Pasadena, CA 91101-2024
626-578-9315
eyaa@artsed411.org
http://www.artsed411.org/projects/eya.stm

Young artists pursuing postsecondary training in visual arts are eligible to apply for Emerging Young Artist Awards of up to $5,000 per year for four years. Applicants must be high school seniors, demonstrate financial need, and reside in the state of California. For further details and to download an application, visit the alliance's Web site. If you don't reside in California, visit http://www.kennedy-center.org/education/kcaaen/statealliance/aaemem.html for a list of programs in your state or search the Web using keywords such as "state art councils" or "state art alliances."

Collegeboard.com
http://apps.collegeboard.com/cbsearch_ss/welcome.jsp

This testing service (PSAT, SAT, etc.) offers a scholarship search engine that features scholarships (not all fashion-related) worth nearly $3 billion. You can search by specific major and a variety of other criteria.

CollegeNET
http://www.collegenet.com

CollegeNET features 600,000 scholarships (not all fashion-related) worth more than $1.6 billion. You can search by keyword (such as "fashion") or by creating a personality profile of your interests.

Council of Fashion Designers of America
1412 Broadway, Suite 2006
New York, NY 10018-9250
212-302-1821
info@cfda.com
http://www.cfda.com

College students who are studying fashion design or related fields may apply for merit-based scholarships from the Council. Applicants must be completing their junior year of college. Contact the council for more information.

Daughters of the American Revolution (DAR)
Scholarship Committee
1776 D Street, NW
Washington, DC 20006-5303
202-628-1776
http://www.dar.org/natsociety/edout_scholar.cfm

General scholarships are available to students who have been accepted or who are currently enrolled in a college or university in the United States. Selection criteria include academic excellence, commitment to field of study, and financial need; applicants need not be affiliated with DAR. A scholarship program is also available for Native American students. Contact DAR for more information.

Fashion Institute of Design & Merchandising
800-624-1200
http://www.fidm.edu/features/dot/dot.html

The institute—which has campuses in Los Angeles, Irvine, San Francisco, and San Diego, California—offers a variety of fashion-related associate degrees, including fashion design, merchandise marketing, and footwear design. Many financial aid options are available to students planning to attend or currently attending the institute. One of its programs is a scholarship competition that requires entrants to submit projects such as "creating a promotional plan for a major fashion retailer; designing a poster for a trendy line of sportswear; creating an ideal bedroom for a young couple; or designing a new clothing line." Contact the institute for more information.

Fashion Institute of Technology (FIT)
Seventh Avenue at 27th Street
New York, NY 10001-5992
212-217-7999
FITinfo@fitnyc.edu
http://www.fitnyc.edu/html/dynamic.html

FIT offers associate, bachelor's, and master's degrees in 30 fashion-related fields, including fashion design, fashion merchandising management, global fashion management, menswear, photography, and visual art management. The institute offers financial aid to its students. Visit its Web site for more information.

FastWeb
http://fastweb.monster.com
FastWeb features 600,000 scholarships (not all fashion-related) worth more than $1 billion. To use this resource, you will need to register (free).

Florida Alliance for Arts Education/Arts for a Complete Education
The First Lady's Arts Recognition Scholarship Program
402 Office Plaza
Tallahassee, FL 32301-2757
866-919-3223
http://www.faae.org

High school seniors planning to major in the arts are eligible to apply for Arts Recognition Scholarships. Applicants must be Florida residents. Visit the alliance's Web site for more information. If you don't reside in Florida, visit http://www.kennedy-center.org/education/kcaaen/statealliance/aaemem.html for a list of programs in your state or search the Web using keywords such as "state art councils" or "state art alliances."

Foundation for the Carolinas
217 South Tryon Street
Charlotte, NC 28201-3201
704-973-4500
http://www.fftc.org

The foundation administers more than 70 scholarship funds that offer awards to undergraduate and graduate students pursuing study in the arts, graphic arts, and other disciplines. Visit its Web site for a searchable list of awards.

Golden Key International Honor Society
621 North Avenue, NE, Suite 100
Atlanta, GA 30308-2857
800-377-2401
http://www.goldenkey.org

Golden Key is an academic honor society that offers its members "opportunities for individual growth through leadership, career development, networking, and service." It awards more than $400,000 in scholarships annually through 17 different award programs. Membership in the society is selective; only the top 15 percent of college juniors and seniors—who may be pursuing education in any college major—are considered for membership by the organization. There is a one-time membership fee of $60 to $65. Contact the society for more information.

GuaranteedScholarships.com
http://www.guaranteed-scholarships.com

This Web site offers lists (by college) of scholarships, grants, and financial aid (not all fashion-related) that "require no interview, essay, portfolio, audition, competition, or other secondary requirement."

Hawaii Community Foundation
1164 Bishop Street, Suite 800
Honolulu, HI 96813-2810
808-537-633
scholarships@hcf-hawaii.org
http://www.hawaiicommunityfoundation.org/scholar/scholar.php

The foundation offers a variety of scholarships for high school seniors and college students planning to study or currently studying art (including drawing and photography) and other majors in college. Applicants must be residents of Hawaii, demonstrate financial need, and plan to attend a two- or four-year college. Visit the foundation's Web site for more information and to apply online.

Hispanic College Fund (HCF)
1717 Pennsylvania Avenue, NW, Suite 460
Washington, DC 20006-2614
800-644-4223
hcf-info@hispanicfund.org
http://www.hispanicfund.org

The Hispanic College Fund, in collaboration with several major corporations, offers a variety of scholarships for high school seniors and college students planning to study or currently studying fashion and other majors. Applicants must be Hispanic, live in the United States or Puerto Rico, and have a GPA of at least 3.0 on a 4.0 scale. Contact the HCF for more information.

Illinois Career Resource Network
http://www.ilworkinfo.com/icrn.htm

Created by the Illinois Department of Employment Security, this useful site offers a great scholarship search engine, as well as detailed information on careers (including fashion). You can search for scholarships based on fashion majors (such as fashion design and fashion merchandising) and keyword. This site is available to everyone, not just Illinois residents; you can get a password by simply visiting the site. The Illinois Career Information System is just one example of sites created by state departments of employment security (or departments of labor) to assist students with financial- and career-related issues. After checking out this site, visit the Web site of your state's department of labor to see what it offers.

Illinois Institute of Art at Chicago
350 North Orleans Street
Chicago, IL 60654-1975
800-351-3450
http://www.ilic.artinstitutes.edu/financialaid.asp

The institute offers associate of applied science degrees in fashion merchandising and fashion production and bachelor's of fine arts degrees in fashion design and fashion marketing and management. Approximately 80 percent of its students received some form of financial aid in 2004. Some of the institute's financial aid programs are competition-based. Visit the institute's Web site for more information. (Note: There are 31 Art Institutes located throughout the United States and Canada. Visit http://www.aii.edu for a complete list.)

International Academy of Design and Technology–Chicago
One North State Street, Suite 500
Chicago, IL 60602-3302
312-980-9200
http://www.iadtchicago.edu

The academy offers associate and bachelor's degrees in fashion design. Scholarships ranging from $250 to $10,000 are available to students who are planning to attend or currently attending the academy. Visit the academy's Web site for more information. (Note: Academies are also located in Tampa, Florida, and Toronto, Canada.)

Iowa Arts Council
Attn: Sarah Ekstrand, Arts Resources Coordinator
600 East Locust
Des Moines, IA 50319-0290
515-281-4657
Sarah.Ekstrand@iowa.gov
http://www.iowaartscouncil.org/funding/scholarship-for-the-arts/index.shtml?id=2

Iowa high school seniors who demonstrate proven artistic ability in visual arts and other areas are eligible to apply for $1,000 to $2,000 Iowa Scholarships for the Arts. Applicants must be Iowa residents and plan to attend full time an accredited college or university in Iowa. Contact the Arts Resources coordinator for more information. If you don't reside in Iowa, visit http://www.kennedy-center.org/education/kcaaen/statealliance/aaemem.html for a list of programs in your state or search the Web using keywords such as "state art councils" or "state art alliances."

Maryland State Arts Council
175 West Ostend Street, Suite E
Baltimore, MD 21230-3792
410-767-6555
msac@msac.org
http://www.msac.org

Maryland artists who are at least 18 years of age may compete for Maryland State Arts Council Individual Artist Awards of $1,000, $3,000, and $6,000. Applicants must be Maryland residents. Students who are currently enrolled in art degree programs are not eligible. Visit the Council's Web site for details. If you don't reside in Maryland, visit http://www.kennedy-center.org/education/kcaaen/statealliance/aaemem.html for a list of programs in your state or search the Web using keywords such as "state art councils" or "state art alliances."

Minnesota State Arts Board
Park Square Court, Suite 200
400 Sibley Street
Saint Paul, MN 55101-1928
800-866-2787
msab@arts.state.mn.us
http://www.arts.state.mn.us

The board offers $2,000 to $6,000 grants to Minnesota artists and photographers at various stages in their careers. Visit its Web site for more information. If you don't reside in Minnesota, visit http://www.kennedy-center.org/education/kcaaen/statealliance/aaemem.html for a list of programs in your state or search the Web using keywords such as "state art councils" or "state art boards."

National Endowment for the Arts (NEA)
1100 Pennsylvania Avenue, NW
Washington, DC 20004-2501
202-682-5400
http://arts.endow.gov/grants

Congress established the NEA in 1965 to support excellence in the arts. It offers grants to artists and arts organizations working in the following art disciplines: arts education, design, folk and traditional arts, media arts, multidisciplinary, and visual arts. Visit the NEA Web site for a detailed list of available programs.

National Foundation for Advancement in the Arts
Arts Recognition and Talent Search
444 Brickell Avenue, P-14
Miami, FL 33131-2403
800-970-ARTS
http://www.nfaa.org

High school seniors and other 17- and 18- year-old artists are eligible to apply for $3 million in college scholarships via the Arts Recognition and Talent Search. Individual cash awards range from $100 to $10,000. Categories include photography, visual arts, and nonfiction writing. Applicants are not judged against one another, but judged based on standards of excellence established by the foundation. Visit the foundation's Web site for more information.

Nebraska Arts Council
1004 Farnam Street
Omaha, NE 68102-1839
800-341-4067
http://www.nebraskaartscouncil.org

The council offers Individual Artist Fellowships of $1,000 to $5,000 to Nebraska visual artists (drawing, photography, etc.), performing artists, and writers (non-fiction, etc.) of superior ability. Contact the council for more information. If you don't reside in Nebraska, visit http://www.kennedy-center.org/education/kcaaen/statealliance/aaemem.html for a list of programs in your state or search the Web using keywords such as "state art councils" or "state art alliances."

New York Foundation for the Arts
155 Avenue of the Americas, 14th Floor
New York, NY 10013-1507
212-366-6900, ext. 217
nyfaafp@nyfa.org
http://www.nyfa.org

Artists residing in New York State are eligible for two types of financial aid from the foundation. Artists' Fellowships are $7,000 cash awards that are offered in 16 artistic disciplines, including photography and drawing (applications are accepted in eight of these categories each year). Special Opportunity Stipends are offered to help individual artists from all disciplines "take advantage of unique opportunities that will significantly benefit their work or career development." Awards range from $100 to $600. Visit the foundation's Web site to download an application and obtain more information.

North Dakota Council on the Arts
1600 East Century Avenue, Suite 6
Bismarck, ND 58503-0649
701-328-7592
jwebb@state.nd.us
http://www.state.nd.us/arts/grants/grants.htm

The council awards $2,500 Individual Artist Fellowships to practicing artists (including photographers) residing in North Dakota. Visit the Council's Web site for more information. If you don't reside in North Dakota, visit http://www.kennedy-center.org/education/kcaaen/statealliance/aaemem.html for a list of programs in your state or search the Web using keywords such as "state art councils" or "state art alliances."

Oklahoma Visual Arts Coalition
PO Box 54416
Oklahoma City, OK 73154-1416
405-232-6991
http://www.ovac-ok.org/artinfogrants.html

The coalition offers grants and awards to Oklahoma artists who are at least 18 years old and not attending a degree program in visual arts. Awards range from $2,500 to $5,000. Contact the coalition for more information. If you don't reside in Oklahoma, visit http://www.kennedy-center.org/education/kcaaen/statealliance/aaemem.html for a list of programs in your state or search the Web using keywords such as "state art councils" or "state art alliances."

O'More College of Design
423 South Margin Street
Franklin, TN 37064-2816
615-792-4254
http://www.omorecollege.edu/admissions.html

The O'More College of Design offers a bachelor of fine arts in fashion design and merchandising. It provides academic, departmental, and financial need-based scholarships to its students. Contact the college for more information.

Sallie Mae
http://www.collegeanswer.com

This Web site offers a scholarship database of more than 2.4 million awards (not all fashion-related) worth more than $14 billion. You must register (free) to use the database.

Savannah College of Art and Design
PO Box 2072
Savannah, GA 31402-2072
800-869-7223
admissions@scad.edu
http://www.scad.edu/admission/financial/financial_aid/guide/index.cfm

The college offers degree programs in 27 fields, including fashion, illustration, metals and jewelry, and photography. Financial aid is available to students. Contact the college for more information.

Scholarship America
4960 Viking Drive, Suite 110
Edina, MN 55435-5314
800-279-2083
http://www.scholarshipamerica.org

This organization works through its local Dollars for Scholars chapters in 41 states and the District of Columbia. To date, it has awarded more than $1 billion in scholarships to more than one million students. Visit Scholarship America's Web site for more information.

Scholarships.com
http://www.scholarships.com

Scholarships.com offers a free college scholarship search engine (although you must register to use it) and financial aid information.

Scholastic
c/o Alliance For Young Artists And Writers, Inc.
557 Broadway
New York, NY 10012-3999
212-343-6493
a&wgeneralinfo@scholastic.com
http://www.scholastic.com/artandwritingawards

Student artists and writers in grades 7 through 12 are eligible to apply for Scholastic Art and Writing Awards of up to $10,000. Art categories for graduating high school seniors include drawing, photography, animation, mixed media, painting, art portfolio, ceramics and glass, computer art, design, digital imagery, photography portfolio, sculpture, printmaking, and video and film. Writing categories for graduating high school seniors include journalism, dramatic script, humor, novel writing, personal essay/memoir, poetry, science fiction/fantasy, short story, short short story, general writing portfolio, and nonfiction portfolio. More than $20 million in scholarships have been awarded since the awards were founded in 1923. Visit Scholastic's Web site for a detailed overview of the various awards, competition levels, and application instructions.

United Negro College Fund (UNCF)
8260 Willow Oaks Corporate Drive
PO Box 10444
Fairfax, VA 22031-8044
http://www.uncf.org/scholarships

Visitors to the UNCF Web site can search for thousands of scholarships and grants, many of which are administered by the UNCF. High school seniors and undergraduate and graduate students are eligible. The search engine allows you to search by major, state, scholarship title, grade level, and achievement score.

Vermont Alliance for Arts Education (VAAE)
PO Box 327
Fairlee, VT 05045-0327
802-333-4468
vaae@valley.net
http://www.vaae.org

High school seniors planning to major in the arts are eligible to apply for VAAE Student Arts Scholarships. Applicants must be Vermont residents. Visit the alliance's Web site for more information. If you don't reside in Vermont, visit http://www.kennedy-center.org/education/kcaaen/statealliance/aaemem.html for a list of programs in your state or search the Web using keywords such as "state art councils" or "state art alliances."

World Studio Foundation
200 Varick Street, Suite 507
New York, NY 10014-7041
212-366-1317
scholarshipcoordinator@worldstudio.org
http://www.worldstudio.org

High school seniors and college students planning to pursue or currently pursuing undergraduate or graduate degrees in the fine or commercial arts, design, or architecture are eligible to apply for scholarships from the foundation. Scholarships are offered in many areas, including fashion design, fine arts, graphic design, illustration, and photography. Applicants must demonstrate financial need; preference will be given to applicants from underrepresented minority groups. Visit the foundation's Web site for more information on scholarship amounts and to download an application.

Look to the Pros

The following professional organizations offer a variety of materials, from career brochures to lists of accredited schools to salary surveys. Many also publish journals and newsletters that you should become familiar with. Some have annual conferences that you might be able to attend. (While you may not be able to attend a conference as a participant, it may be possible to cover one for your school or even your local paper, especially if your school has a related club.)

When contacting professional organizations, keep in mind that they all exist primarily to serve their members, be it through continuing education, professional licensure, political lobbying, or just keeping up with the profession. While many are strongly interested in promoting their profession and providing information about it to the general public, these professional organizations are busy with many other activities. Whether you call or write, be courteous, brief, and to the point. Know what you need and ask for it. If the organization has a Web site, check it out first: what you're looking for may be available there for downloading, or you may find a list of prices or instructions, such as sending a self-addressed stamped envelope with your request. Finally, be aware that organizations, like people, move. To save time when writing, first confirm the address, preferably with a quick phone call to the organization itself: "Hello, I'm calling to confirm your address. . . "

❑ THE SOURCES

American Apparel and Footwear Association
1601 North Kent Street, Suite 1200
Arlington, VA 22209-2105
800-520-2262
http://www.apparelandfootwear.org/

This national trade organization represents apparel, footwear, and other sewn-products companies. Visit its Web site for a list of publications about the apparel and footwear industry.

American Institute of Graphic Arts
164 Fifth Avenue
New York, NY 10010-5901
212-807-1990
http://www.aiga.org

This professional association for graphic designers and related professionals is dedicated to the promotion of excellence in the field of design through publications, exhibitions, competitions, seminars, conferences, and student membership. Visit the Ideas for Students section at its Web site to read "Graphic Design: A Career Guide," which covers educational and career requirements. The section also offers tips on presenting your portfolio and avoiding resume mistakes.

American Purchasing Society
PO Box 256
Aurora, IL 60506-0256
630-859-0250
http://www.american-purchasing.com

The society represents purchasing professionals in a variety of industries, including fashion. Visit its Web site for a glossary of common purchasing terms and information on certification.

Association of Stylists and Coordinators
18 East 18th Street, #5E
New York, NY 10003-1933
info@stylistsasc.com
http://www.stylistsasc.com

Visit the association's Web site to review portfolios of fashion stylists.

Council of Fashion Designers of America
1412 Broadway, Suite 2006
New York, NY 10018-9250
212-302-1821
info@cfda.com
http://www.cfda.com

This is a professional membership organization for fashion and accessory designers. Visit the council's Web site for industry news and information on scholarships, internships, and its Visiting Designers program, which allows undergraduate students to talk with designers and have their work critiqued.

Custom Tailors and Designers Association of America
19 Mantua Road
Mt. Royal, NJ 08061-1006
856-423-1621
http://www.ctda.com

This is a professional membership organization for custom tailors and designers.

Fashion Group International, Inc.
8 West 40th Street, 7th Floor
New York, NY 10018-3902
212-302-5511
info@fgi.org
http://www.fgi.org

Fashion Group International is a nonprofit association of more than 6,000 professionals in the fashion, apparel, accessories, beauty, and home industries. Visit its Web site for information on college student membership, career counseling resources, and student career days.

International Association of Clothing Designers and Executives
835 Northwest 36th Terrace
Oklahoma City, OK 73118-7104
405-602-8037
newyorkiacde@cox.net
http://www.iacde.com

This is a professional membership organization for clothing designers and executives. Visit its Web site to read news about the association and developments in the industry.

International Modeling and Talent Association
http://www.imta.com

This is an organization of training centers for models and talent. Visit its Web site for information on modeling careers, competitions, and annual conventions.

National Association of Schools of Art and Design (NASAD)
11250 Roger Bacon Drive, Suite 21
Reston, VA 20190-5248
703-437-0700
info@arts-accredit.org
http://nasad.arts-accredit.org

Contact the NASAD for information on accredited arts programs. You can search a free online version of its list of accredited institutions by name, city, and/or state. (For a small fee, you can search a more extensive version of the list.) Additionally, visit the FAQ: Students, Parents, Public section for useful information on preparing to study art or design in college, applying for financial aid, and accreditation.

National Endowment for the Arts (NEA)
1100 Pennsylvania Avenue, NW
Washington, DC 20004-2501
202-682-5400
http://arts.endow.gov

Congress established the NEA in 1965 to support excellence in the arts. It offers grants to artists and arts organizations, as well as various community-based programs. Visit its Web site for more information.

National Retail Federation
325 7th Street, NW, Suite 1100
Washington, DC 20004-2818
800-673-4692
http://www.nrf.com/content/default.asp?folder=foundation&file=main.htm&bhcp=1

The federation represents more than 1.4 million U.S. retail establishments and more than 23 million employees (approximately 20 percent of American workers). Visit the Web site of its foundation for information on retail careers and certification and links to professional organizations.

Professional Photographers of America
229 Peachtree Street, NE, Suite 2200
Atlanta, GA 30303-1608
800-786-6277
csc@ppa.com
http://www.ppa.com

Contact this organization for information on certification, training, competitions, and *Professional Photographer* magazine.

7th on Sixth
IMG
22 East 71st Street
New York, NY 10021-4975
212-253-2692
info@thonsixth.com
http://www.7thonsixth.com

7th on Sixth offers venues for designers to showcase their latest fashions. Contact the organization for more information on volunteer opportunities.

Society of Illustrators
128 East 63rd Street
New York, NY 10021-7303
212-838-2560
info@societyillustrators.org
http://www.societyillustrators.org

This national institution promotes and stimulates interest in the art of illustration by offering exhibits, lectures, educational programs, and social exchange. Contact the society for information on student membership, career information, and a list of postsecondary art schools that offer courses, continuing education, or majors in the applied arts of illustration, cartooning, graphic design, or visual communications.

Student Photographic Society
229 Peachtree Street, NE, Suite 2200
Atlanta, GA 30303-1608
866-886-5325
http://www.studentphoto.com

Contact the society for information on student membership, careers, and competitions.

Index

Entries and page numbers in **bold** indicate major treatment of a topic.

D

G

H

I

J

K

L

M

N

O

P